THE UNI
CAMEL

How Ambitious Entrepreneurs Can Build and
Scale a Billion-Dollar Business in the GCC

Abdulrahman AlHammadi

PASSIONPRENEUR®
PUBLISHING

Print: 978-1-76124-262-5
E-book: 978-1-76124-264-9
Hardback: 978-1-76124-263-2

Publishing information
Publishing and design facilitated by Passionpreneur Publishing
A division of Passionpreneur Organization Pty Ltd
ABN: 48640637529

Melbourne, VIC | Australia
www.passionpreneurpublishing.com

CONTENTS

DEDICATION

To all ambitious entrepreneurs in the GCC who dare to dream big and have the courage to pursue those dreams. Your vision and determination are shaping the future of our region.

ACKNOWLEDGMENTS

I would like to express my deepest gratitude to the visionary leaders of the GCC countries whose forward-thinking policies have created an environment where innovation can thrive. To the entrepreneurs who shared their stories with me, the investors who offered their insights, and the mentors who guided my journey—thank you for your contributions to this book and to the ecosystem we are all building together.

INTRODUCTION

A SYMBOL FOR OUR TIME

The camel is not just an animal—it's a *symbol*. It's a symbol of the GCC. It's a symbol of resilience. It's a symbol of endurance. It's a symbol of adaptation. It's a symbol of survival in harsh conditions.

For decades, the startup world has been obsessed with unicorns. Unicorns are mythical creatures—rare, magical, impossible. They represent a certain vision of success: rapid growth, disruption, scale at any cost, exit for billions.

But the unicorn is not a symbol for the GCC. The unicorn is fragile. It's imaginary. It's not built for the desert.

The camel is different. The camel is real. The camel is built for the desert. The camel survives. The camel endures. The camel carries generations.

The camel is the symbol for what we're building in the GCC.

This is the Uni-Camel, a billion-dollar company that's built like a camel—resilient, enduring, adapted to the GCC, carrying the region forward.

In these pages, you'll learn how to build one.

PART 1

Think Like a Billion-Dollar Founder

Entrepreneurs seeking extraordinary success require more than a strong personal brand. They have certain qualities that give them the edge to leverage their unique insights to act on opportunities and gain credibility. The ability to think big, embrace risk and maintain resilience are key elements of a billion-dollar founder. This mindset shift is crucial for overcoming obstacles and seizing opportunities.

In Part 1, we cover the essential qualities and critical skills that successful founders must develop to achieve the kind of success that leads to building billion-dollar enterprises.

CHAPTER 1

REPOSITION YOURSELF

Establishing Authority in Your Industry

When I started in business fifteen years ago, I was just another entrepreneur with big dreams but limited connections. Like many of you reading this book, I found myself questioning whether I truly belonged in the high-stakes world of tech startups. Who would listen to my ideas? Why would investors trust me with their capital? How could I possibly compete with established players who seemed to have it all figured out?

I remember sitting in countless coffee shops across Dubai and Riyadh with my co-founder, rehearsing my pitch before meetings, wondering if I was just fooling myself. My first attempts at raising capital were met with polite nods and empty promises of 'We'll wait for a committee decision.' My product demos often ended with lukewarm responses.

I watched as other entrepreneurs with different ideas struggled to get funding.

The turning point came when I realized something fundamental: in the GCC's rapidly evolving ecosystem, expertise isn't just about what you know—it's about how you position yourself and communicate your vision. I wasn't failing because my ideas lacked merit; I was failing because I hadn't established myself as an authority worth listening to.

The moment everything changed for me was during a regional tech conference in Dubai. After yet another rejection, I found myself sitting alone, scrolling through LinkedIn and seeing announcements of funding rounds for startups that seemed like mine. Frustration mounting, I struck up a conversation with a seasoned investor sitting nearby. What he told me transformed my approach entirely: 'In this region, we don't just invest in ideas—we invest in determined experts who can execute them.'

That simple statement hit me like a thunderbolt. I had been positioning myself as someone with a good idea, when I should have been positioning myself as the expert who could uniquely deliver on that idea. The GCC market, with its unique blend of traditional values and futuristic vision, doesn't just reward innovation—it rewards authoritative innovation.

When I began repositioning myself as an authority in my field—speaking at events, publishing insights on regional platforms, and demonstrating deep knowledge of both global trends and local nuances—everything shifted. The same investors who had previously dismissed me were suddenly reaching out. Partners who hadn't returned my calls were proposing collaborations.

This transformation wasn't magic—it was strategic expert positioning. And in the GCC's relationship-driven business culture, it makes all the difference.

The results were immediate and transformative. Within a year of my mindset shift, I had secured seed funding. The journey was about pivoting my product to a position that would solve real problems, and how I positioned myself in relation to it.

Why should you care about my journey? Because the GCC startup ecosystem is at a unique inflection point. The region's governments are pouring unprecedented resources into fostering innovation, creating a once-in-a-generation opportunity for entrepreneurs who know how to position themselves effectively. My story isn't exceptional—it's replicable. And throughout this book, I'll show you exactly how to replicate it.

My expertise comes not just from my own entrepreneurial journey, but from having mentored several startups across the GCC region, helping them navigate the unique challenges of this market. I've worked directly with innovation hubs gaining insider knowledge of what decision-makers are really looking for.

My book helps ambitious, visionary, and determined entrepreneurs who are aspiring to build and scale up their business ideas in the GCC. Through simple guidelines and a structured system, I'll show you how to position yourself as an authority in your field, build meaningful relationships with investors and partners, and navigate the unique opportunities and challenges of this dynamic region. By the time you finish reading, you'll have a clear roadmap for building a billion-dollar Uni-Camel business in the GCC—starting with establishing yourself as the expert who deserves to lead it.

This journey begins with understanding the mindset shift required to see beyond conventional limitations and recognize the extraordinary potential of the GCC market. In the next chapter, we'll explore how to develop the big-picture thinking that separates billion-dollar founders from the rest, and why the GCC represents the perfect canvas for your ambitious vision.

CHAPTER 2

MINDSET SHIFT

Your Billion-Dollar Mission Starts Here

THE NEXT WAVE OF FUNDING

Can you genuinely envision building a billion-dollar enterprise within the next three to five years?

Does that sound like an audacious dream, perhaps even an unattainable fantasy in a global market often perceived as saturated and fiercely competitive? What if I told you that not only is it possible, but the conditions in a specific, rapidly evolving region are uniquely primed to support such ambition?

The GCC is not just an emerging market; it is a frontier of unparalleled opportunity for visionary entrepreneurs ready to think big and act decisively. This isn't about chasing fleeting trends; it's about understanding a fundamental shift in the global economic and technological landscape, and positioning yourself to ride the crest of this transformative wave.

DEFINING THE UNI-CAMEL

By the end of this chapter, you will gain a profound understanding of why the GCC represents a fertile arena for building a 'Uni-Camel'—a resilient, billion-dollar venture adapted to thrive in this unique ecosystem. We will dismantle common misconceptions about global market saturation and illuminate the distinct advantages the GCC offers, from robust governmental support to a tech-savvy, youthful population eager to embrace innovation. You will learn about the critical mindset shift required to recognize and seize these opportunities, moving from a localized perspective to a global vision anchored in regional strengths. You will discover how to identify the key pillars of the GCC's potential and equip yourself with the foundational understanding needed to embark on your billion-dollar mission with clarity and conviction. We will explore the burgeoning next wave of funding and how it aligns with the region's ambitious growth trajectory, setting the stage for you to not just participate, but lead.

EXPOSING MISCONCEPTIONS AND UNDERSTANDING THE CURRENT GLOBAL SITUATION

Many aspiring entrepreneurs, particularly those with global ambitions, often look towards traditional powerhouses like the United States or rapidly growing economies like China. While these markets have undoubtedly produced numerous success stories, the current reality presents a more nuanced picture. The USA, for instance, is an incredibly competitive arena. Thousands of tech companies, many with substantial backing and established market presence, vie for consumer attention and investor capital. Breaking through the noise and securing the necessary funding to scale can be an arduous, often demoralizing, journey. The sheer density of innovation means that even brilliant ideas can struggle to gain traction without exceptional execution and significant resources.

Similarly, while China's economic growth has been phenomenal, its major tech sectors are now largely dominated by established giants. A decade ago, the landscape might have offered more accessible entry points for new ventures, but today, navigating its complex regulatory environment and competing with deeply entrenched incumbents presents formidable challenges. The dream of easily tapping into its vast consumer base often collides with the harsh realities of market saturation and intense local competition. These markets, while large, are not necessarily the most fertile ground for every new billion-dollar idea, especially for those seeking rapid growth and supportive ecosystems from the outset.

In stark contrast, the GCC region—encompassing Saudi Arabia, the United Arab Emirates, Kuwait, Qatar, Bahrain, and Oman—emerges as a landscape of fresh opportunity. It is a market that is not only actively seeking innovation but is also designing a a supportive framework to attract and nurture it. The narrative here is not one of fighting for scraps in an overcrowded space, but of co-creating the future in a region hungry for technological advancement and economic diversification. Governmental support is not a mere buzzword; it is a tangible reality, with nations like Saudi Arabia and the UAE spearheading initiatives to become global hubs for technology and entrepreneurship. They are not just passively waiting for founders to arrive; they are actively rolling out the red carpet, offering incentives, and streamlining processes to attract the brightest minds and the most promising ventures. This fundamental difference in market dynamics and governmental posture is the first crucial element in the mindset shift required to see the GCC for what it truly is: a launchpad for the next generation of Uni-Camels.

PROVIDING A NEW PERSPECTIVE: THE GCC'S WELCOMING EMBRACE

Imagine an environment where your innovative ideas are not only welcomed but actively sought after, where substantial technological and financial support is readily available, and where the ecosystem is geared towards helping you develop and scale your business. This isn't a utopian fantasy; it's the emerging reality within the GCC. Wouldn't you prefer to build your empire in a place that actively wants you to win, rather than one where you are just another contender in an overcrowded arena? This is the core of the AHA! moment for many forward-thinking entrepreneurs. The GCC offers a unique confluence of factors that create an exceptionally supportive environment for ambitious startups. An opportunity to build the Uni-Camel.

When we look at the support systems, a clear hierarchy emerges, though all member states are moving in a positive direction. Saudi Arabia and the UAE are undoubtedly the powerhouses, with the largest economies and the most aggressive and well-funded national strategies to foster innovation and attract foreign investment. Their vision extends beyond mere economic growth: they are aiming to become global leaders in key technological sectors. Following closely are countries like Kuwait, Qatar, and Bahrain. While smaller in scale, they are equally committed to creating supportive ecosystems, often carving out niches and offering specialized incentives to attract specific types of ventures. Oman, with its unique cultural heritage and strategic location, is also increasingly focusing on developing its startup scene, particularly in areas like tourism tech, logistics, and sustainable technologies.

Beyond governmental initiatives, the demographic and technological landscape of the GCC is a critical component of its appeal. The region boasts a young, highly educated, and digitally native population. This demographic is not just a consumer base; it's an engine for innovation and early adoption. There's a palpable hunger for new technologies and services, a willingness to embrace change that significantly lowers the barriers to market entry for many tech-driven businesses. This rapid tech adaptation, coupled with a strong governmental push and a welcoming attitude towards new businesses, creates a fertile ground where innovative ideas can take root and flourish at an accelerated pace. The mindset shift involves recognizing that the traditional centers of innovation are no longer the only, or even the best, options. The GCC is not just catching up; it's positioning itself to leapfrog, and it's inviting ambitious founders to be part of that journey.

THE UNI-CAMELS ALREADY THRIVING

The theoretical appeal of the GCC is compelling, but the true validation of its potential lies in the tangible successes already emerging from the region. We are not talking about distant future possibilities; we are witnessing the rise of Uni-Camels—billion-dollar companies—that have been nurtured and scaled within this very ecosystem. These aren't isolated incidents; they are indicative of a broader trend, a testament to the fertile ground the GCC provides for ambitious ventures. Companies across various sectors, from e-commerce and fintech to logistics and digital services, have already achieved significant valuations and are demonstrating the immense scalability possible in the region.

Consider the trajectory of companies like Careem, the ride-hailing service that was acquired by Uber for a staggering $3.1 billion, showcasing the potential for massive exits. Look at Kitopi, a leading cloud kitchen platform, which achieved unicorn status by addressing the evolving food delivery landscape. In the fintech space, companies like Tabby and Tamara have rapidly grown to become major players in the Buy Now, Pay Later (BNPL) market, attracting substantial international investment and demonstrating the region's appetite for innovative financial solutions. Souq.com, an e-commerce giant, was acquired by Amazon, further highlighting the strategic importance and growth potential of the GCC's digital economy.

These are not just success stories; they are data points proving the hypothesis that the GCC is a market where billion-dollar businesses can be built and can thrive. They underscore the combination of a receptive consumer base, a supportive regulatory environment, and access to capital that characterizes the region. These pioneering companies have paved the way, demonstrating that the path to Uni-Camel status in the GCC is not just a theoretical possibility but a well-trodden road for those with the right vision, strategy, and execution. Their success serves as powerful evidence that the mindset shift towards viewing the GCC as a prime destination for ambitious entrepreneurs is not just optimistic, but realistic and data-driven. The next wave of funding is increasingly recognizing this, and the stories of these thriving Uni-Camels are a call to founders worldwide: the GCC is ready for your billion-dollar idea.

ROADMAP: KEY PILLARS FOR YOUR BILLION-DOLLAR GCC MISSION

Understanding the immense potential of the GCC is one thing; strategically navigating its landscape to build a billion-dollar Uni-Camel is another. This requires a clear roadmap, a set of guiding pillars that will form the bedrock of your mindset and operational approach. These pillars are actionable principles derived from the unique characteristics of the GCC market and the success stories that have emerged from it. Let's delve into these key steps that will illuminate your path:

1. **Deeply Internalize the GCC Vision 2030 (and Beyond)**: Across the GCC, particularly in Saudi Arabia (Vision 2030) and the UAE (Centennial 2071), ambitious national visions are driving unprecedented economic transformation. These are not mere policy documents; they are comprehensive blueprints for diversifying economies away from oil, fostering innovation, developing world-class infrastructure, and creating vibrant societies. As an entrepreneur, your first step is to immerse yourself in these visions. Understand their core objectives, the key sectors they prioritize (such as technology, tourism, entertainment, renewable energy, and advanced manufacturing), and the specific initiatives and incentives being rolled out to support them. Aligning your business idea with these national priorities can unlock significant advantages, including access to funding, streamlined regulatory approvals, and strategic partnerships. This isn't about opportunistically fitting in; it's about genuinely contributing to a larger national and regional ambition. The mindset shift here is from being a standalone entity to becoming an integral part of a transformative journey.

2. **Embrace Hyper-Localization with a Global Mindset**: While the GCC shares common cultural and economic threads, each member state also possesses unique nuances, consumer behaviors, and regulatory

landscapes. A one-size-fits-all approach is unlikely to yield optimal results. Therefore, a crucial pillar is to adopt a strategy of hyper-localization. This means tailoring your products, services, marketing messages, and even your business operations to the specific context of each target market within the GCC. However, this localization must be underpinned by a global mindset. Your operational standards, technological infrastructure, and long-term ambitions should be world class.. Think globally, act locally. This involves investing in local talent, understanding cultural sensitivities, and adapting your value proposition to resonate with local needs, all while building a scalable and internationally competitive business. The Uni-Camel thrives by being deeply rooted in its local environment while having the strength and vision to compete on a global stage.

3. **Prioritize Digital Transformation and Tech-Driven Innovation**: The GCC is a region characterized by high internet penetration, widespread smartphone adoption, and a youthful population that is exceptionally tech-savvy. Digital transformation is not just a trend; it is the primary engine of growth and innovation across all sectors. Whether your business is in fintech, e-commerce, health-tech, edtech, or even traditional industries, leveraging technology is non-negotiable. This pillar emphasizes the need to build tech-driven solutions, embrace data analytics to understand customer behavior, utilize digital marketing channels effectively, and continuously innovate to stay ahead of the curve. The GCC governments are

actively promoting the adoption of emerging technologies like AI, IoT, blockchain, and robotics. Founders who can harness these technologies to solve real-world problems and create value will find a receptive market and a supportive ecosystem. The mindset here is to be a digital-first enterprise, constantly seeking ways to enhance efficiency, customer experience, and scalability through technology.

4. **Cultivate Strategic Partnerships and Ecosystem Engagement**: The business landscape in the GCC is often relationship-driven. Building strong networks and cultivating strategic partnerships can significantly accelerate your growth trajectory. This involves engaging with various stakeholders in the ecosystem, including government agencies, local conglomerates, venture capital firms, angel investors, industry associations, and other startups. These partnerships can provide access to market insights, distribution channels, funding opportunities, and a pool of talented individuals. Actively participate in industry events, join accelerator and incubator programs, and seek mentorship from experienced entrepreneurs and business leaders in the region. The Uni-Camel doesn't operate in isolation; it thrives by being an active and collaborative member of the ecosystem, leveraging collective strengths to achieve its ambitious goals. The mindset shift is from a purely competitive stance to one that embraces collaboration and co-creation for mutual benefit.

5. **Focus on Talent Development and Human Capital**: While technology is a critical enabler, human capital is the ultimate driver of success. As you scale your Uni-Camel, attracting, developing, and retaining top talent will be paramount. The GCC is investing heavily in education and skills development, but the demand for specialized skills, particularly in technology and innovation, often outstrips supply. This pillar underscores the importance of creating an attractive employer brand, offering competitive compensation and benefits, fostering a positive and inclusive work culture, and investing in continuous learning and development for your team. Consider strategies for tapping into both local and international talent pools. Building a diverse and highly skilled team that is aligned with your vision and values is essential for navigating the complexities of the GCC market and achieving sustainable growth. The mindset here is to view your people as your most valuable asset and to create an environment where they can thrive and contribute their best work.

6. **Navigate the Regulatory and Legal Landscape with Diligence**: Each GCC country has its own set of laws, regulations, and licensing requirements. Navigating this landscape can be complex, but it is crucial for ensuring compliance and mitigating risks. This pillar emphasizes the need for due diligence and seeking expert legal and financial advice. Understand the requirements for business registration, foreign ownership, taxation, data protection, and intellectual property rights in each

target market. While governments are actively working to streamline these processes and create more business-friendly environments, it is essential to stay informed about any changes and to ensure that your operations are fully compliant. Building a strong foundation of legal and regulatory compliance will not only protect your business but also enhance your credibility with investors and partners. The mindset here is to be proactive and meticulous in managing legal and regulatory obligations, viewing them not as obstacles but as essential components of building a sustainable and reputable enterprise.

These pillars provide a strategic framework for your billion-dollar mission in the GCC. They are interconnected and require a holistic and adaptive approach. By internalizing these principles and consistently applying them to your business strategy, you can significantly enhance your chances of building a resilient and highly successful Uni-Camel in this dynamic and promising region.

SUMMARY
- **Recalibrate Your Perspective**: Shift your mindset towards the GCC's immense potential as a launchpad for billion-dollar ambitions.
- **Challenge Misconceptions**: Notice unique hurdles of markets like the USA and China compared to the GCC.
- **Supportive Ecosystem**: The GCC's rapidly evolving ecosystem is characterized by:
  - Proactive governmental support
  - A young, tech-savvy demographic

- A genuine desire to foster innovation
- Leadership from nations like Saudi Arabia and the UAE.

Success Stories: Proof of existing Uni-Camels (e.g., Careem, Kitopi, Tabby, Tamara) that billion-dollar valuations are attainable in the GCC.

Multi-Pillar Roadmap: Outline a strategic framework for operational execution:
- Aligning with national visions like Saudi Vision 2030
- Embracing hyper-localization with a global outlook
- Prioritizing digital transformation
- Cultivating strategic ecosystem partnerships
- Focusing on talent development
- Navigating the regulatory landscape.

Building Resilience: By implementing these pillars, you are architecting a resilient Uni-Camel poised for extraordinary growth and impact.

Funding Opportunities: Recognize that the next wave of funding is increasingly aware of the GCC's unique opportunities.

Call to Action: It is time to be at the forefront of this exciting new chapter in global entrepreneurship.

Having grasped the vast potential of the GCC and the fundamental mindset shift required to tap into it—we now turn our attention inward. A grand vision and a supportive environment are essential, but they are only part of the equation.

The success of any Uni-Camel ultimately rests on the capabilities, resilience, and strategic acumen of its founder.

What does it truly take to lead such an ambitious venture?

Next, we will delve into the essential attributes and competencies you must cultivate to navigate the challenging yet rewarding journey of building your Uni-Camel. We will explore the decision-making process, the leadership qualities, and the unwavering determination that define the architects of the world's most impactful companies.

CHAPTER 3

FOUNDER SKILLS

What It Takes to Be a Billion-Dollar Founder

What are the core skills and traits that separate those who dream from those who build billion-dollar realities?

Let's move from the 'why' to the 'how,' by dissecting the essential founder skills needed to thrive in the dynamic GCC landscape.

THE CORE OF A FOUNDER

At the heart of every Uni-Camel, every billion-dollar success story, lies a founder, or a founding team, driven by more than just profit. These individuals are a unique breed, characterized by a distinct set of intrinsic qualities and approaches to problem-solving. They are not simply businesspeople; they are architects of value, visionaries who see possibilities where others see obstacles.

Their core identity is rooted in an insatiable curiosity and an almost obsessive drive to understand people. They are less interested in abstract ideas or fleeting trends and more captivated by the intricacies of human behavior, the unmet needs, and the persistent pain points that individuals and businesses grapple with daily. This profound empathy and user-centric focus mean they don't chase pre-conceived notions of what a good idea is; instead, they meticulously solve real, tangible problems. Their ventures are born from a deep understanding of a specific challenge and a relentless pursuit of an elegant, effective solution.

Furthermore, billion-dollar founders are models of resilience and resourcefulness. The entrepreneurial journey, especially one aimed at such ambitious heights, is invariably fraught with setbacks, failures, and moments of profound doubt. What sets these founders apart is their ability to not just withstand these pressures but to learn from them, adapt, and emerge stronger. They are resourceful in their approach, capable of achieving significant milestones with limited means, and unwavering in their focus on long-term value creation over short-term gains or superficial metrics. They understand that building a Uni-Camel is a marathon, not a sprint, requiring sustained effort, strategic patience, and an unshakeable belief in their mission.

It is equally important to debunk common myths and misconceptions that often cloud the perception of what it takes to reach this echelon of success:

1. One prevalent myth is that you need to be a technical guru to build a billion-dollar tech company. While a strong understanding of technology is undoubtedly an asset, it is not a prerequisite for founding success. Many of the world's most successful Uni-Camels were co-founded by non-technical visionaries who excelled in leadership, strategy, market understanding, and team building. They understood the problem deeply and had the acumen to assemble a team with the requisite technical expertise, often bringing on a technical co-founder or an early, highly skilled Chief Technology Officer. The critical factor is not personal coding ability but the capacity to lead a technically proficient team towards a common goal.

2. Another pervasive myth is the notion that the idea has to be perfect before you start. This pursuit of perfection can be paralyzing, leading to inaction and missed opportunities. The reality, as exemplified by countless successful startups, is that most groundbreaking ideas evolve significantly through a process of iteration, market feedback, and continuous learning. The initial concept is merely a starting point; the real magic happens in the relentless cycle of building, measuring, and learning, adapting the offering based on real-world user interactions and data.

3. Finally, there's the misconception that you need to raise a lot of money from day one. While capital is undeniably important, an early over-reliance on external funding can sometimes be detrimental, leading to premature scaling, loss of focus, or dilution of vision. Many Uni-Camels began their journeys by bootstrapping, operating with extreme leanness, and focusing intensely on achieving product-market fit and generating early revenue. This approach not only instills financial discipline but also ensures that the business model is validated and the value proposition is clear before seeking large-scale investment.

BECOMING MORE

The action point for aspiring Uni-Camel founders is to: 'Get curious. Start learning. Ask better questions.' Cultivate an unquenchable thirst for knowledge about your industry, your potential customers, and the evolving market dynamics. Challenge assumptions, seek diverse perspectives, and learn to ask insightful questions that uncover the latent needs and unarticulated desires of your target audience.

Beyond the inherent qualities and the debunking of myths, becoming the founder of a billion-dollar Uni-Camel involves a profound internal transformation and the cultivation of specific, high-impact traits. This isn't merely about acquiring new skills; it's about fundamentally rewiring your approach to challenges, opportunities, and leadership.

In Chapter 2, we discussed the crucial mindset shift required to perceive the GCC not as a peripheral market but as a central hub of opportunity. A founder must undergo a personal mindset shift. This is a transition far more demanding than any career change; it is a metamorphosis from an employee or manager, operating within established frameworks, to a visionary leader, an architect of the new, and a calculated risk-taker. It means stepping away from the comfort of predictability and embracing uncertainty and ambiguity not as threats, but as the very fabric of the entrepreneurial landscape. This personal evolution requires an unwavering belief in one's vision, even when faced with skepticism, and the courage to make bold decisions in the absence of complete information. It's about developing a comfort level with the unknown and the resilience to navigate the inevitable turbulence of building something from scratch.

KEY TRAITS OF BILLION-DOLLAR FOUNDERS

Resilience: This is perhaps the most tested trait on the entrepreneurial battlefield. Resilience is the capacity to bounce back, stronger and wiser, from the inevitable failures, rejections, and setbacks that litter the path to building a Uni-Camel. It's about maintaining an unyielding motivation and perseverance when adversity strikes, whether it's a product launch that falls flat, a critical funding round that doesn't close, or a key team member who departs unexpectedly. In the GCC context, resilience might also involve navigating new and evolving market dynamics, adapting to different cultural business practices, or patiently working through potential bureaucratic hurdles. It's the inner fortitude that keeps a founder pushing forward when others might succumb to pressure. Resilience is not an innate gift but a muscle built through consistent exposure to challenges and a conscious effort to learn from each experience.

Clarity (of Vision and Purpose): A billion-dollar founder must possess an almost luminous clarity regarding their company's vision and its underlying purpose. This isn't just about having a good idea; it's about articulating a compelling future state that the company aims to create and explaining why it matters. This clarity must be so profound that it can be communicated effectively and inspiringly to every stakeholder—from the earliest employees and co-founders to potential investors, partners, and, most importantly, customers. In a world filled with distractions and competing priorities, this unwavering clarity acts as a compass, guiding strategic decisions and keeping the entire organization focused on the most critical objectives.

Long-Term Vision: While agility and responsiveness to immediate market conditions are vital, Uni-Camel founders are distinguished by their capacity for long-term thinking. They are not solely focused on quarterly results or immediate gains; they are architecting an enterprise built to last, to scale, and to create enduring impact. This involves understanding the broader socio-economic and technological trends shaping the future, particularly within the GCC, and positioning the company to capitalize on these long-wave opportunities. It means making investments and strategic choices today that may only yield significant returns years down the line.

Decision-Making Under Uncertainty: The entrepreneurial journey is a constant stream of decisions, many of which must be made with incomplete data and under significant time pressure. The ability to make sound judgments in such conditions is paramount. This involves developing frameworks for decision-making, which might include a blend of data-informed analysis, pattern recognition honed through experience, and a well-calibrated intuition. It also requires the courage to make tough calls and to take calculated risks, knowing that not every decision will be perfect but that inaction can be far more detrimental.

Speed of Execution Without Compromising Quality: In today's rapidly evolving markets, particularly in the tech-driven sectors prevalent in the GCC, speed of execution is a significant competitive advantage. The ability to rapidly iterate on products, enter new markets swiftly, and respond to changing customer needs can be the difference between leading the pack and being left behind. However, this speed cannot come at the expense of quality. Uni-Camel founders master the delicate art of balancing rapid execution with the maintenance of high standards in their products, services, and customer experiences. This often involves building agile teams, implementing efficient processes, and fostering a culture that values both velocity and excellence.

Emotional Intelligence (EQ) and Leadership: A founder's ability to lead is intrinsically linked to their emotional intelligence. EQ encompasses self-awareness (understanding one's own strengths, weaknesses, and emotional triggers), self-regulation (managing one's impulses and adapting to changing situations), empathy (understanding and sharing the feelings of others), and social skills (building rapport, managing relationships, and inspiring action). These skills are crucial for building, motivating, and leading high-performing teams, which are the lifeblood of any scaling venture. Effective leadership involves not just directing tasks but also fostering a positive and inclusive company culture, managing conflict constructively, and inspiring loyalty and commitment.

Persuasion and Storytelling for Investor and Team Alignment: A founder is, in many ways, the chief storyteller of their organization. The ability to craft and deliver a compelling narrative around the company's vision, its value proposition, and its potential impact is essential for attracting investment, recruiting top talent, and aligning the entire team around shared goals. This goes beyond mere presentation skills; it involves understanding the audience, tailoring the message, and connecting on an emotional level. Effective storytelling can transform a complex business idea into a relatable and inspiring vision that resonates with investors, employees, and customers alike.

SUMMARY

Becoming a billion-dollar founder (a Uni-Camel) is a challenging journey that requires a unique blend of intrinsic qualities and cultivated skills. Along with that, it demands an unwavering commitment to a long-term vision.

- **Mindset Shift**: Embrace uncertainty and ambiguity as opportunities for growth and innovation.
- **Skill Development**: Focus on critical skills in:
  - Resilience
  - Decision-making
  - Clarity of Purpose
  - Long-term Vision
  - Speed of Execution
  - EQ in Leadership
  - Storytelling.
- **Market Understanding**:
  - A youthful, tech-savvy population
  - A rapidly evolving economic landscape.
- **Action Steps**:
  - Assess your strengths and areas for growth against the discussed traits
  - Identify where you excel and where you need development.
- **Curiosity Building**:
  - Identify three pressing problems in your target market
  - Spend a week researching these problems:
    - Talk to potential customers
    - Read industry reports
    - Understand pain points you might solve
  - Document your findings to reveal missed opportunities.
- **Decision-Making Practice**:
  - Make decisions with incomplete information
  - Practice calculated risk-taking in smaller contexts.

- **Storytelling Development**:
  - ◦ Craft and refine your vision
  - ◦ Communicate it clearly and passionately in under two minutes.
- **Building Resilience**:
  - ◦ Seek new challenges that push you beyond your comfort zone
  - ◦ Embrace failures as learning opportunities
  - ◦ Extract valuable lessons from setbacks.
- **Long-Term Focus**: Strengthening your resilience now will pay dividends throughout your entrepreneurial journey.

Having explored the essential skills and mindset of a billion-dollar founder, we now turn our attention to the specific market where these attributes can be most effectively deployed. Next, we'll dive deep into the distinctive characteristics that make the Gulf Cooperation Council region an unparalleled opportunity for ambitious entrepreneurs. We'll examine the economic landscape, demographic advantages, technological readiness, and governmental support systems that collectively create a fertile ground for Uni-Camels to flourish. Understanding this market context is crucial—even the most skilled founder needs the right environment to maximize their chances of success. Let's explore why the GCC might just be the perfect canvas for your billion-dollar vision.

PART 2

The GCC Opportunity

The Market That Wants You to Win

This section delves into the unique advantages of the GCC market. We start with the region's supportive ecosystem, youthful demographic, and favorable regulations, positioning it as an ideal landscape for ambitious entrepreneurs. We then showcase success stories from companies like Talabat, Tabby, and Tamara, illustrating achievable billion-dollar valuations. Following on, we examine emerging trends in AI, robotics, fintech, healthtech, edtech, and deeptech, highlighting opportunities for innovation. Finally, drawing inspiration from global unicorns, we reveal practical lessons that aspiring founders can apply in the GCC context.

This provides a comprehensive roadmap for aspiring founders, empowering them to harness the potential of the GCC market and build successful, impactful ventures.

CHAPTER 4

GCC POTENTIAL

A Unique and Fresh Market to Build Your Empire

A DREAMLAND THAT IS REALITY

Imagine a global landscape where the very mention of starting a new venture conjures images of intense, cutthroat competition, where customer acquisition costs are soaring, and where market saturation seems to be the norm.

Now, contrast that with a region actively seeking innovation, where the cost of reaching and engaging a tech-adaptive populace is comparatively lower, and where accelerated growth is not just a possibility but an observable trend. This isn't a hypothetical scenario; it's the unfolding reality of the Gulf Cooperation Council (GCC)—a unique and fresh market poised to become a global hub for technological advancement and entrepreneurial success.

We will explore the proactive role governments across the region are playing in fostering innovation, creating an environment where adapting and adopting new technologies is not just encouraged but actively facilitated. You will learn how to identify and leverage the key emerging technological trends—from AI and robotics to fintech, healthtech, and edtech—that are shaping the future of the GCC and presenting unprecedented opportunities for disruption and value creation.

For any aspiring Uni-Camel founder, the question of 'What's in It for Me?' when considering the GCC is not just relevant; it's fundamental. Why should you, with your billion-dollar ambitions and global perspective, focus your energies and resources on this specific cluster of nations in the Arabian Gulf? The answer lies in a confluence of strategic advantages that are increasingly rare in the global startup ecosystem.

Think about the last time you encountered a truly unsaturated market, a place where the demand for innovative solutions significantly outstrips the current supply, where governmental bodies are not obstacles but active partners in your growth, and where a young, tech-savvy population is eager to embrace new technologies. This is the GCC today. While other regions may offer larger consumer bases or more established tech hubs, the GCC presents a unique combination of factors that make it an exceptionally attractive proposition for ambitious entrepreneurs.

The GCC nations, particularly Saudi Arabia and the UAE, are not just passively waiting for innovation to happen; they are actively driving it. Their national visions, such as Saudi Vision 2030 and the UAE Centennial 2071, are comprehensive blueprints for economic diversification, technological advancement, and societal development. These visions are backed by substantial government resources, creating an environment where adapting and adopting new technologies is encouraged and actively facilitated. This proactive governmental support translates into tangible benefits for startups, including access to funding, streamlined regulatory processes, and a willingness to embrace disruptive innovation.

Furthermore, the GCC boasts a young, affluent, and digitally native population. This demographic is eager to adopt new technologies and has the disposable income to fuel rapid market growth. The region's high mobile penetration rates and increasing internet connectivity create a fertile ground for digital-first businesses. Unlike more mature markets where incumbents often dominate, the GCC offers a landscape where new entrants can quickly gain traction and scale, especially if they can provide solutions that cater to local needs and preferences.

Understanding the GCC's potential requires a deeper dive into its specific characteristics and the opportunities they present. This section will explore key sectors and strategies for success in this dynamic region.

a. AI & Robotics: Enhancing Efficiency and Innovation in Business Operations

The GCC nations are making substantial investments in Artificial Intelligence (AI) and robotics, viewing them as critical enablers for economic diversification and enhanced global competitiveness. This isn't just about futuristic showcases; it's about practical applications that drive efficiency and create new value streams. Opportunities abound for startups that can develop and deploy AI-powered solutions in areas such as smart city management (optimizing traffic flow, energy consumption, public safety), advanced logistics and supply chain optimization (a crucial sector given the GCC's role as a global trade hub), AI-driven diagnostics and personalized medicine in healthcare, and intelligent automation in customer service and back-office operations. Robotics is also gaining traction, not just in industrial manufacturing but also in services, hospitality, and even construction. Startups that can offer AI solutions tailored to regional needs, perhaps addressing Arabic language processing challenges or specific industry verticals like oil and gas or Islamic finance, will find a receptive and supportive environment.

b. Fintech Revolution: The Transformation of Financial Services through Digital Payments

The fintech sector in the GCC is experiencing explosive growth, driven by a combination of factors: a young, digitally savvy population with high smartphone penetration; strong governmental support for cashless economies and financial innovation; and a relatively underdeveloped traditional banking landscape in certain segments, creating space for nimble disruptors. The success of Buy Now, Pay Later (BNPL) platforms like Tabby and Tamara, which have rapidly achieved unicorn status, is a testament to the market's appetite for innovative financial solutions. Opportunities extend far beyond BNPL. Digital wallets, mobile payment systems, challenger banks offering specialized services, regtech solutions that help financial institutions navigate complex compliance requirements, and Islamic fintech products aligned with Sharia principles are all areas with significant growth potential. The drive towards financial inclusion, coupled with the desire for more seamless and personalized financial experiences, means that startups offering user-centric, secure, and efficient fintech solutions are well-positioned for success.

c. Healthtech Evolution: The Rise of Digital Healthcare Solutions and Telemedicine

GCC governments are prioritizing the enhancement of healthcare quality, accessibility, and efficiency, leading to a surge in demand for healthtech solutions. The COVID-19 pandemic further accelerated the adoption of digital health services, particularly telemedicine. Opportunities are plentiful for startups focusing on teleconsultations, remote patient monitoring, AI-powered diagnostic tools, electronic health records (EHR) systems tailored to regional needs, and digital pharmacy services. There's also a growing interest in wellness apps and wearable technologies that promote preventative healthcare. With significant governmental investment in healthcare infrastructure and a growing awareness among the population about health and wellness, the healthtech market is poised for substantial expansion. Startups that can provide culturally sensitive, technologically advanced, and cost-effective solutions have the potential to make a significant impact and achieve considerable scale.

d. EdTech & Digital Learning: Revolutionizing Education through Technology

The GCC has a predominantly young population, creating a massive demand for quality education at all levels. Furthermore, the region's economic diversification efforts necessitate a focus on reskilling and upskilling the workforce to meet the demands of future industries. This has fueled a boom in the Edtech sector. Opportunities range from K–12 online learning platforms and personalized tutoring apps to vocational training programs, corporate e-learning solutions, and immersive learning experiences using VR/AR. There is a particular need for content that is localized, culturally relevant, and aligned with the evolving skill requirements of the GCC job market. Startups that can offer engaging, effective, and accessible digital learning solutions, perhaps focusing on in-demand skills like coding, data science, or digital marketing, can tap into a vast and growing market.

e. Deeptech Advancements: AI, Blockchain, Other Disruptive Innovations

While AI has been mentioned, the broader category of Deeptech—encompassing fundamental technological breakthroughs—presents another layer of opportunity. This includes areas like blockchain technology, which offers significant potential beyond cryptocurrencies, such as enhancing supply chain transparency, securing digital identities, and streamlining trade finance. The Internet of Things (IoT) is another critical area, with applications in smart cities, industrial automation, and connected logistics. Quantum computing, while still in its early stages, is also on the radar, with potential applications in areas like drug discovery, materials science, and financial modeling. For founders with a strong R&D focus and the ability to translate complex technologies into commercially viable solutions, the GCC offers an environment increasingly open to supporting such ambitious ventures.

The GCC region presents a unique and compelling opportunity for ambitious entrepreneurs. Its combination of governmental support for innovation, a young and tech-savvy population, and a rapidly diversifying economy creates a fertile ground for building and scaling billion-dollar Uni-Camels. Key sectors like AI, fintech, healthtech, and edtech are experiencing significant growth, driven by strategic national visions and a desire to become global leaders in these fields. Success in the GCC requires a deep understanding of local market dynamics, cultural nuances, and the ability to adapt and innovate rapidly.

IDEAS WORTH BUILDING

If you are an ambitious entrepreneur with a disruptive idea, the GCC should be high on your list of potential markets. The time to act is now. Begin by researching the specific needs and opportunities within your chosen sector, connect with local industry experts and potential partners, and consider participating in regional accelerator programs or industry events. The journey to building a Uni-Camel is challenging, but the rewards for those who succeed in the GCC can be immense. Embrace the opportunity, and you may find yourself at the forefront of the next wave of global innovation.

Having explored the vast potential and emerging technological frontiers of the GCC, it's time to see these opportunities in action. In the next chapter, we will dive into inspiring GCC-specific narratives. We will examine how pioneering companies like Talabat revolutionized food delivery, and how fintech disruptors like Tabby and Tamara captured the imagination of a new generation of consumers. By dissecting their strategies, their challenges, and their triumphs, we can extract practical lessons and invaluable insights to inform your own path to building a billion-dollar Uni-Camel in this dynamic and promising region. Get ready to learn from the best and discover how to turn your vision into a reality in the GCC.

SUMMARY

Key Points on the GCC's Potential and Opportunities

- **Understanding the GCC**:
  - Dive into specific characteristics and opportunities within the region.
  - Explore key sectors and strategies for success.
- **AI & Robotics**:
  - Significant investments in AI and robotics for economic diversification.
  - Opportunities in:
    - Smart city management
    - Logistics and supply chain optimization
    - AI-driven healthcare solutions
    - Intelligent automation in various sectors
    - Startups addressing regional needs, such as Arabic language processing, will thrive.
- **Fintech Revolution**:
  - Explosive growth driven by:
    - A young, digitally savvy population
    - Government support for financial innovation
    - Gaps in the traditional banking landscape.
  - Opportunities include:
    - Digital wallets and mobile payment systems
    - BNPL platforms and challenger banks
    - Regtech and Islamic fintech products.

- **Healthtech Evolution**:
  - Increased demand for digital healthcare solutions, accelerated by COVID-19.
  - Opportunities in:
    - Telemedicine and remote patient monitoring
    - AI-powered diagnostics and EHR systems
    - Wellness apps and wearables.
  - Government investment and public awareness are driving growth.
- **Edtech & Digital Learning**:
  - High demand for quality education due to a young population and economic diversification.
  - Opportunities range from K–12 platforms to vocational training and corporate e-learning.
  - Focus on localized and culturally relevant content is essential.
- **Deeptech Advancements**:
  - Opportunities in blockchain, IoT, and quantum computing.
  - Potential applications in supply chain transparency, digital identities, and industrial automation.
  - Founders with R&D focus can thrive in this supportive environment.
- **Unique GCC Opportunity**:
  - Government support, a tech-savvy population, and a diversifying economy create fertile ground for billion-dollar ventures.
  - Success requires understanding local market dynamics and cultural nuances.

- **Call to Action for Entrepreneurs**:
  - ○ Research specific needs in your sector and connect with local experts.
  - ○ Consider participating in regional accelerator programs and events.
  - ○ Embrace the opportunity to innovate and lead in the GCC.

CHAPTER 5

SUCCESS STORIES

Talabat, Tabby, Tamara

Now, we transition from the theoretical potential and strategic overviews to the tangible proof. It is one thing to understand that a market is promising; it is another entirely to witness that promise actualized through concrete, inspiring examples. By examining the paths of Talabat, Tabby, and Tamara, we move from understanding the landscape to learning from those who have successfully conquered its peaks, extracting actionable lessons and irrefutable evidence of the GCC's viability for your own billion-dollar aspirations.

LEARN FROM THE UNI-CAMELS

Consider these figures for a moment: **Talabat**, a name now synonymous with food delivery across the Middle East, achieved a staggering $6 billion valuation through its IPO within just eight years of its strategic acquisition. **Tabby**, a trailblazer in the Buy Now, Pay Later (BNPL) space, recently secured a monumental $3.3 billion in a funding round, signaling immense investor confidence. Hot on its heels, **Tamara**, another BNPL powerhouse with a strong Saudi Arabian focus, garnered a $1 billion funding round.

These are not abstract numbers; they are resounding testaments to the rapid, large-scale success that is not just possible but is actively being realized within the GCC. These are the proven market facts that should ignite the ambition of every aspiring Uni-Camel founder looking for a dynamic and rewarding ecosystem.

We will deconstruct the remarkable journeys of three iconic regional success stories:

Talabat, the food delivery giant that originated in Kuwait and was later acquired by a German company leading to a significant IPO

Tabby, the BNPL innovator that launched from the UAE and rapidly expanded into Saudi Arabia and other GCC nations

Tamara, its formidable KSA-born competitor that has also successfully broadened its reach across Bahrain and Oman.

You will learn how these distinct companies, operating in different yet equally dynamic sectors, each navigated the regional landscape to achieve billion-dollar valuations, on average, within an astonishing five-year timeframe.

For an aspiring Uni-Camel founder, dissecting these GCC success stories is a vital strategic imperative.

Why should these specific narratives—Talabat, Tabby, Tamara—command your attention?

Because they offer irrefutable, localized proof that the billion-dollar dream is attainable within this very market. They transform the potential into palpable reality, providing a GCC-centric roadmap that is often more relevant and actionable than lessons drawn from vastly different global ecosystems like Silicon Valley or Shanghai.

Risk is an inherent part of any entrepreneurial journey. The founders of Talabat, Tabby, and Tamara were not immune to this; they embraced it. They identified opportunities, often inspired by global trends or unmet local needs, and possessed the audacity to pioneer these concepts within the GCC. They demonstrated unwavering commitment, the courage of a risk-taker, and the foresight of a visionary—qualities that are consistently highlighted as essential for entrepreneurial triumph. Their journeys underscore that success in the GCC is not about replicating global models verbatim, but about intelligently adapting them, understanding local nuances, and persevering through unique regional challenges.

The GCC, due to its less saturated markets in certain tech verticals, strong governmental backing, and eager consumer base, can indeed offer a more fertile ground for well-executed ideas to take root and flourish rapidly. These success stories serve as powerful evidence of this enhanced potential, demonstrating that with the right approach, the odds can be more favorable here than in older, more crowded arenas. Learning from their triumphs and tribulations provides a playbook rich in practical wisdom, directly applicable to your own Uni-Camel ambitions in the Gulf.

To truly internalize the lessons from the GCC market, we must move beyond acknowledging success to meticulously deconstructing it. Each story, while unique, contributes to a broader understanding of what it takes to build a Uni-Camel in this dynamic region.

a. Talabat: The Food Delivery Pioneer Who Redefined Convenience

The story of Talabat is a cornerstone of GCC entrepreneurial folklore, a testament to first-mover advantage coupled with tenacious market development. Originating in Kuwait in 2004, Talabat (which translates to 'orders' in Arabic) ventured into a relatively nascent online food delivery market. At the time, the concept of ordering meals through a digital platform was far from mainstream in the region. The initial challenge was significant: no one offered this service, and the company struggled trying to convince the market to expand. This struggle involved building a technology platform and, more crucially, educating both restaurants and consumers about the benefits of online ordering and delivery. It required immense perseverance to change established habits, convincing restaurants to partner and customers to trust a new way of accessing their favorite meals.

Talabat's early growth was characterized by a grassroots effort to build a network of partner restaurants and a loyal customer base in Kuwait. The key was demonstrating tangible value: for restaurants, it was access to a wider customer base and increased order volume; for consumers, it was convenience, variety, and ease of use. As the model proved successful in Kuwait, Talabat embarked on a strategic expansion across the GCC, entering key markets like Saudi Arabia and the UAE. This expansion was not without its complexities, requiring adaptation to local logistical challenges, payment preferences, and consumer behaviors in each new territory.

The turning point in Talabat's journey, catapulting it into the global spotlight, was its acquisition by Rocket Internet in 2015 for a reported $170 million—at the time, one of the largest tech exits in the Middle East. (The company was transferred to German multinational Delivery Hero one month later, which took over Rocket Internet's food delivery business.) Talabat, which started small, ultimately benefitted from the IPO. Indeed, under Delivery Hero's stewardship, Talabat continued its aggressive growth, leveraging the parent company's global expertise and resources while retaining its strong regional brand identity. The subsequent IPO of Delivery Hero, with Talabat as a significant asset, underscored the immense value created. The journey from a struggling Kuwaiti startup, reportedly initiated with a modest investment (in the context of the original founder, though details of early funding can be complex and involve multiple stages and founders, including the narrative of a later founder acquiring it 'from small founder for a cheap price' and then building it with 'commitment'), to a multi-billion-dollar entity within a global food delivery empire is a powerful illustration of the GCC's potential to scale ventures to international significance. Talabat's success lay in identifying a fundamental consumer need (convenience in food ordering), relentlessly building the ecosystem to serve that need, and strategically scaling across a receptive regional market before attracting global interest.

b. Tabby: The BNPL Disruptor Riding the Wave of Digital Commerce

Tabby's ascent in the GCC's burgeoning fintech landscape is a story of impeccable timing, deep market understanding, and experienced leadership. Launched in the UAE in 2019, Tabby entered the Buy Now, Pay Later (BNPL) sector just as e-commerce was experiencing exponential growth in the region, a trend further accelerated by the COVID-19 pandemic. Hosam Arab, Tabby's CEO, brought invaluable insights from his time at Souq.com (later acquired by Amazon), including a profound understanding of GCC consumer behavior, e-commerce dynamics, and the challenges of digital payments.

Tabby identified a critical gap in the market: while consumers were increasingly shopping online, traditional credit penetration was not as high as in Western markets, and there was a cultural preference among younger demographics for more flexible, interest-free payment solutions. BNPL offered an elegant answer, allowing shoppers to split their purchases into manageable installments without incurring interest charges, thereby increasing affordability and boosting conversion rates for merchants. Tabby's value proposition was clear: for consumers, it was financial flexibility and empowerment; for merchants, it was increased sales, larger basket sizes, and access to a wider customer base.

Their growth strategy involved rapidly forging partnerships with a wide array of online and offline retailers across the UAE and then strategically expanding into Saudi Arabia, the GCC's largest market, followed by other countries like Kuwait and Egypt. Securing significant funding rounds, including the recent one that valued the company at $3.3 billion, has been instrumental in fueling this expansion, investing in technology, and building brand awareness. Tabby's success factors include its user-friendly platform, seamless integration with merchant checkouts, a strong focus on risk management, and its ability to cater to the preferences of the region's young, digitally native population. They effectively tapped into the GCC's high smartphone penetration and the growing comfort with digital financial services, demonstrating how a well-executed fintech solution addressing a clear consumer pain point can achieve massive scale in a supportive ecosystem.

c. Tamara: The KSA-Born BNPL Powerhouse with Regional Ambitions

Tamara, launched in Saudi Arabia in late 2020, emerged as a formidable player in the BNPL space, showcasing the depth of opportunity within this vertical and the potential for strong, locally-founded companies to thrive. Similar to Tabby's founder, Abdulmajeed Alsukhan, co-founder and CEO of Tamara, brought prior entrepreneurial experience from his involvement with Nana, a Saudi-based online grocery delivery platform. This local expertise and understanding of the Saudi market, in particular, proved to be a significant asset.

Tamara's core offering, like Tabby's, revolves around providing shoppers with flexible, interest-free installment payment options. Their KSA-first strategy allowed them to deeply penetrate the Kingdom's large and rapidly growing e-commerce market, tailoring their services to local consumer preferences and regulatory nuances. They quickly gained traction by partnering with major retailers in Saudi Arabia and then expanded their operations to other GCC countries, including the UAE, Kuwait, and Bahrain.

The company's ability to secure substantial funding, including a round that valued it at $1 billion, highlights the strong investor appetite for promising fintech ventures in the region. Tamara's success can be attributed to its strong execution, its focus on building a robust merchant network, its user-centric approach, and its deep understanding of the Saudi consumer.

The emergence of both Tabby and Tamara, achieving Uni-Camel status in a relatively short period, underscores the significant market demand for BNPL services in the GCC and the region's capacity to support multiple major players in high-growth sectors, fostering a competitive yet rewarding environment for innovation.

These three narratives—Talabat's pioneering journey in food delivery, and Tabby and Tamara's rapid conquests in the BNPL space—collectively paint a vibrant picture of entrepreneurial success in the GCC. They demonstrate that with the right idea, a deep understanding of the local market, strong execution, and the ability to leverage the region's unique advantages, building a billion-dollar Uni-Camel is not just a distant dream but an achievable reality.

While the narratives themselves are powerful, supporting materials can further illuminate the scale and nature of these GCC successes. Visualizing their growth trajectories and distilling core founder themes provides deeper insights.

FUNDING AND VALUATION TRAJECTORIES (CONCEPTUAL)

While precise, private funding details are often confidential until officially announced, the public domain provide strong indicators of the rapid value creation by companies like Tabby and Tamara. Conceptually, one could chart this:

- **Talabat**: Initial modest investment → Growth & Expansion → $170M Acquisition (2015) → Continued growth under Delivery Hero → Contributes to Delivery

Hero's multi-billion dollar market cap (effective $6B valuation impact cited).

- **Tabby (Founded 2019)**: Seed funding $5M USD as a starting point → Series A → Series B → Significant later-stage rounds leading to $3.3B valuation (by ~2023/2024).
- **Tamara (Founded 2020)**: Seed funding also 5M USD → Subsequent rounds leading to $1B valuation (by ~2023/2024).

These timelines, typically spanning just 3–5 years from significant scaling to Uni-Camel status for Tabby and Tamara, highlight the accelerated growth achievable in the GCC's receptive market. This rapid scaling is a key attraction for founders and investors alike.

FOUNDER INSIGHTS & THEMES

Talabat's Evolution: Firstly, the ability to spot undervalued assets or struggling early ventures and transform them with renewed vision and commitment. Secondly, the sheer power of perseverance in overcoming initial market resistance. Thirdly, the strategic wisdom of aligning with a global player (Delivery Hero) for further scaling and a successful exit/public market validation. This highlights that the founder journey can involve different roles at different stages—from originator to scaler to strategic partner.

Serial Entrepreneurship (Tabby & Tamara): Both Tabby's founder (ex-Souq.com) and Tamara's founder (ex-Nana) are highlighted as serial entrepreneurs. This is a powerful theme. Their prior ventures, even if not all were billion-dollar exits themselves, provided invaluable experience, market knowledge, networks, and credibility. They learned from past successes and failures, enabling them to identify new opportunities (like BNPL) with greater acuity and execute more effectively. This underscores the value of accumulated entrepreneurial capital.

Starting Capital: The mention of '5M USD' as a starting point for ventures like Tabby and Tamara (likely referring to early significant seed/Series A rounds rather than initial angel investment) indicates that while substantial, the initial capital required to gain traction in the GCC for a strong idea can be within reach, especially for experienced founders. The key is demonstrating a clear path to product-market fit and scalability.

These supporting elements reinforce the idea that success in the GCC is driven by a combination of market opportunity, founder acumen (including experience, commitment, and vision), and the ability to attract and deploy capital effectively to achieve rapid growth.

The remarkable journeys of Talabat, Tabby, and Tamara are not isolated incidents—they are indicative of broader patterns and conditions conducive to success in the GCC. However, capitalizing on these conditions requires a specific mindset and approach from the founder.

If you have a great idea, and experience in the technology sector, then the GCC will be the place to support you to achieve your goal. This is a crucial point. The GCC ecosystem is increasingly sophisticated in its ability to identify and back promising ventures, especially those led by founders with a proven track record or deep domain expertise. A compelling idea, validated by market research and a clear understanding of local needs, coupled with the technical and business acumen to execute, will find receptive ears among investors and support organizations.

While the GCC talent pool is rapidly maturing, it's true that in certain specialized, cutting-edge tech roles, the depth of experience might not yet match that of more established global tech hubs. However, this can be an advantage in several ways. Firstly, it presents an opportunity for visionary founders to attract, mentor, and shape emerging talent, building highly loyal and dedicated teams. Secondly, the competition for top-tier experienced talent, while growing, might be less intense than in Silicon Valley, potentially allowing startups to build strong core teams more effectively. The key is to invest in training and development and to create an inspiring work environment.

FACTORS THAT CONTRIBUTE TO GROWTH

The most significant condition for success, echoed in the Talabat story and the broader theme of innovation, is the ability to learn from global models and adapt them to the local GCC context. This is not about blind imitation but intelligent adaptation. Food delivery, BNPL, and e-commerce were not invented in the GCC. However, the successful GCC Uni-Camels in these spaces understood how to tailor these global concepts to regional consumer behaviors, payment preferences, logistical realities, and cultural nuances. This involves more than just translating an app into Arabic; it requires a deep empathy for the local customer and a willingness to iterate the business model to achieve product-market fit within the GCC. The success of these companies proves that a globally proven concept, when thoughtfully localized and executed with excellence, can find immense success in the fresh and dynamic GCC market.

SUMMARY

Key Takeaways from GCC Success Stories

- **Inspiring Examples**: Talabat, Tabby, and Tamara exemplify the immense potential for billion-dollar Uni-Camels in the GCC.
- **Talabat's Journey**:
  ○ Pioneered a new category in food delivery.
  ○ Scaled from a local Kuwaiti startup to a global empire through resilience and strategic acumen.
- **Tabby and Tamara's Success**:
  ○ Led by experienced entrepreneurs in the Buy Now, Pay Later space.
  ○ Achieved extraordinary valuations rapidly by targeting digitally native consumers.
- **Blueprint for Success**:
  ○ Illustrated the potential of bringing innovative ideas to the GCC.

- ○ Emphasized visionary leadership, understanding local dynamics, and taking calculated risks.
- **Not Just Consumers**: The GCC is becoming a potent creator of its own Uni-Camel success stories, not merely a consumer of global innovation.
- **Lessons for Aspiring Founders**:
  - ○ Use the success of these companies as inspiration and practical guidance.
  - ○ Reflect on how your ideas align with unmet needs and emerging trends in the GCC.
- **Action Steps**:
  - ○ Compare your ideas to the global market and explore their relevance in the GCC.
  - ○ Conduct deep market research and engage with potential customers.
  - ○ Network with local industry players to gain insights and support.
- **Call to Action**:
  - ○ The GCC is ready for the next generation of Uni-Camel founders.
  - ○ Step into the arena with your vision and the lessons learned from these pioneers to lay the foundation for your billion-dollar success story.

Having witnessed the tangible success achieved by visionary founders in the GCC and understanding the market's proven potential, the path forward begins to crystallize. We've seen that it can be done and learned from how others have done it. The next logical step in our journey is to transition from inspiration and market understanding to the practicalities of creation. All these successful ventures began with a core offering, a solution to a problem. This leads us directly to the critical phase of product development.

We will explore how to translate your validated idea into its first tangible form, focusing on the lean strategies and iterative processes that allow you to build, measure, and learn efficiently, ensuring you are creating something the market truly desires before committing to large-scale development— a principle that undoubtedly underpinned the early stages of Talabat, Tabby, and Tamara.

CHAPTER 6

EMERGING TRENDS

AI, Robotics, Fintech, Healthtech, Edtech, Deeptech

Imagine for a moment that you possess the foresight to identify the next seismic shift in technology, the kind of shift that birthed giants like Google, Apple, or Microsoft.

What if the seeds of such a transformation are being sown right now, within the dynamic and ambitious ecosystem of the GCC?

The power to build the next globally recognized Uni-Camel often lies in recognizing and harnessing these nascent yet potent emerging trends before they become mainstream. This chapter is your lens into that future, a future you can actively shape.

Dissecting the success stories of GCC Uni-Camels like Talabat, Tabby, and Tamara, their journeys provided irrefutable proof of the region's market viability and offered a rich tapestry of actionable insights for aspiring founders.

We saw how visionary leadership, coupled with a keen understanding of local dynamics and a commitment to execution, transformed bold ideas into billion-dollar realities. These narratives were not just inspiring; they were instructive, demonstrating that it can be done and offering glimpses into how it was achieved within the unique GCC context.

Now, armed with the wisdom gleaned from these past triumphs, we pivot our gaze towards the horizon. From learning from established successes, we now turn to understanding and anticipating the powerful technological currents that will shape the next wave of Uni-Camels.

By the end of this chapter, you will be empowered to think bigger and embrace broader ideas about the future of technology and business in the GCC. You will gain a strategic overview of the key emerging technological trends—Artificial Intelligence (AI) and robotics, the ongoing fintech revolution, the evolution of healthtech, the transformation in edtech, and the foundational shifts driven by deeptech. We will explore what these technologies are, and their potential impact on the GCC. More importantly, how visionary founders can build innovative, globally competitive businesses around them. This chapter will expand your perspective, encouraging you to look beyond current market offerings and envision the next generation of solutions that will define the industries of tomorrow, originating from the vibrant GCC launchpad.

THE STRATEGIC APPROACH

For an aspiring Uni-Camel founder, a deep and nuanced understanding of emerging technological trends is not a mere academic pursuit; it is a fundamental strategic imperative. Why should you, amidst the myriad demands of building a venture, dedicate significant mental bandwidth to dissecting AI, Robotics, fintech, healthtech, edtech, and deeptech? The answer is to think bigger and out of the box, so that you can lead the industry that you are entering.

In a world of accelerating change, incremental improvements and me-too solutions rarely lead to billion-dollar valuations or lasting market leadership. True Uni-Camel status is often achieved by those who anticipate the trajectory of technological evolution, identify the white spaces where innovation can flourish, and build ventures that are not just current but future-defining. Understanding these emerging trends allows you to move beyond reacting to the present market and start proactively shaping the future one. It equips you to identify untapped opportunities that others might overlook, to develop truly innovative products and services that solve tomorrow's problems today, and to build businesses with strong, defensible competitive advantages rooted in cutting-edge technology.

Furthermore, a profound grasp of these trends is essential for crafting a compelling vision—a vision that can attract top talent, secure significant investment, and inspire customer loyalty. It enables you to articulate what your company does, and why it matters in the grand scheme of technological progress and societal development. By aligning your venture with these powerful currents, you position yourself not as a follower, but as a pioneer. This is about more than just staying relevant; it's about setting the agenda, future-proofing your enterprise, and cultivating the ambition to build a globally impactful company that originates from the supportive and forward-looking ecosystem of the GCC. The insights gained from this exploration are your keys to unlocking transformative ideas and leading the charge in your chosen industry.

To truly harness the GCC's potential as a launchpad for globally significant Uni-Camels, founders must be alert and recognize emerging trends and at the same time develop the vision to innovate within them at a scale that transcends regional boundaries. Learn from giants like Amazon, Apple, Microsoft, Alibaba, and Uber (which notably acquired Careem, a GCC-born Uni-Camel). These companies didn't just participate in trends; they defined them, often starting with a focused solution and relentlessly expanding their scope and impact. The GCC, with its ambition and resources, offers a unique environment to nurture such world-changing ideas.

a. Artificial Intelligence (AI) & Robotics: Beyond Efficiency to Redefinition

While Chapter 4 touched upon AI and robotics for operational efficiency, the true Uni-Camel opportunity lies in creating

AI-first businesses that redefine entire industries or create entirely new product categories. Think beyond chatbots and automation; envision AI that tackles fundamental challenges in areas like sustainable resource management (critical for the GCC), personalized education at a national scale, or breakthroughs in urban planning for the smart cities of the future. The GCC's willingness to invest heavily in AI infrastructure and talent development, coupled with a regulatory environment that is increasingly supportive of innovation, provides fertile ground. For instance, a GCC-born AI company could become a global leader in specialized AI for arid agriculture, or develop ethical AI frameworks that set international standards. Robotics can move beyond industrial applications to areas like assistive technologies for an aging global population or autonomous systems for complex environmental monitoring. The ambition should be to develop proprietary AI algorithms and robotic systems that are not just adopted locally but are sought after globally.

b. Fintech Evolution: Architecting the Future of Finance

The fintech revolution in the GCC has already produced Uni-Camels in areas like BNPL. However, the next wave of opportunity lies in more foundational and globally scalable innovations. Consider the potential for Decentralized Finance (DeFi) solutions tailored to the region's unique regulatory and cultural landscape, including Islamic finance principles. Imagine AI-driven wealth management platforms that democratize access to sophisticated investment strategies for a global clientele, originating from the GCC's established financial hubs. There's immense potential in building next-generation payment infrastructures, perhaps leveraging blockchain for enhanced security and transparency in cross-border transactions, or creating regtech solutions that become the global standard for compliance in emerging markets. The GCC's strategic location and its role as a financial bridge between East and West make it an ideal base for fintech companies with global ambitions. The key is to move beyond replicating existing models to architecting entirely new financial paradigms.

c. Healthtech Futures: From Regional Solutions to Global Impact

GCC governments are heavily invested in transforming their healthcare sectors, creating a demand for innovative healthttech solutions. While telemedicine and digital health records are important, the Uni-Camel potential lies in areas with global implications. Think of AI-powered diagnostic tools that can be deployed in underserved regions worldwide, or research in genomics and personalized medicine that leverages the GCC's diverse population data (with appropriate ethical considerations and data privacy) to make breakthroughs in treating global diseases. There are opportunities in developing advanced HealthTech for preventative care and longevity, addressing global challenges of aging populations. A GCC-based healthtech company could pioneer new models for remote surgical assistance using robotics and AR/VR, or develop platforms for managing global health crises. The focus should be on innovations that not only elevate healthcare standards within the GCC but also offer scalable solutions to pressing global health issues.

d. Edtech Next Generation: Personalized Learning for a Global Audience

The demand for effective and accessible education is a global constant. The GCC's focus on upskilling its youth and workforce creates a strong local market for edtech, but the vision should extend beyond regional needs. Imagine AI-driven personalized learning platforms that adapt to individual student needs at an unprecedented scale, making quality education accessible to millions globally. Consider the development of immersive educational experiences using the metaverse, creating engaging and effective learning environments for complex subjects. There's a vast opportunity in creating lifelong learning platforms that cater to the evolving skill demands of the global digital economy, perhaps specializing in areas where the GCC aims to be a leader, like sustainable energy or advanced technology. An edtech Uni-Camel from the GCC could become a global standard for vocational training in future-critical industries or a leading provider of culturally nuanced educational content for diverse international markets.

e. Deeptech – The Foundational Shifts: Building the Bedrock of Future Industries

Deeptech encompasses technologies that offer significant scientific or engineering breakthroughs, forming the bedrock of future industries. This is where the GCC, with its long-term vision and willingness to make substantial R&D

investments, can truly shine. Beyond AI and blockchain (which have deeptech aspects), consider the potential in areas like quantum computing, which could revolutionize drug discovery, materials science, and complex system optimization. Advanced materials, nanotechnology, biotechnology, and even space technology (given the UAE's ambitious space program) are all fields where foundational IP can be created and nurtured within the GCC. Building a deeptech Uni-Camel requires a long-term perspective, significant investment in research and development, and a focus on creating and protecting intellectual property. The ambition here is not just to build applications but to own the core technologies that will power the next generation of innovation globally. The GCC's sovereign wealth funds and strategic investment arms are increasingly looking to back such transformative, long-horizon ventures.

For founders in the GCC, the lesson from global giants like Amazon or Alibaba is not to copy their specific products, but to emulate their mindset: start with a bold vision, leverage emerging technologies to solve big problems, obsess over the customer, and relentlessly iterate and scale. The GCC provides the resources and the ambition; founders must bring the innovative spark and the global perspective.

To truly build globally competitive companies from the GCC, founders must draw inspiration and strategic insights from existing global giants while also leveraging the unique ambitions and resources of the region.

STORIES OF GCC COMPANIES WITH GLOBAL AMBITIONS/REACH

While the GCC is still maturing in terms of exporting its own tech Uni-Camels on a massive global scale (beyond regional dominance and successful exits like Careem or Talabat to international players), the ambition is undeniably present. Consider companies in sectors:

- **Renewable energy**: e.g. Masdar in the UAE, which have a global footprint and are driven by the GCC's strategic pivot towards sustainability.
- **Logistics**: companies like DP World are global players.
- **Aviation**: Emirates and Qatar Airways have long been global leaders.

While not all are classic venture-backed tech startups, they demonstrate the GCC's capacity to build and operate world-class enterprises. The next wave will likely see more tech-centric companies emerging with similar global ambitions, particularly in areas like fintech, AI applications, and potentially specialized edtech or healthtech solutions tailored for emerging markets worldwide, using the GCC as a highly supportive and well-funded launchpad. The key is to identify sectors where the GCC has a strategic imperative to lead or possesses unique advantages (e.g. energy expertise, capital, a hub for global trade) and build tech-enabled businesses that can scale internationally from that strong foundation.

LEARNING FROM GLOBAL GIANTS — THE KLARNA/PAYPAL METHODOLOGY

Klarna and PayPal are excellent illustrations of a crucial methodology for GCC founders: study global leaders, understand their core value proposition and business model, identify how that model can be adapted or improved for the GCC context (or a new, related niche), and then potentially use that refined model to expand globally.

Klarna (Sweden-based Fintech): Klarna revolutionized online payments in Europe and the US with its innovative 'buy now, pay later' (BNPL) solutions and smooth checkout experiences. A GCC founder looking at Klarna could read reports from 2012–2025 to analyze its customer acquisition strategies, its merchant partnership models, its risk management techniques, and its technology platform. The goal isn't to clone Klarna, but to understand the fundamental consumer needs it addressed (desire for flexible payments, aversion to traditional credit interest for some segments) and the business model innovations it introduced. This understanding can then spark ideas for a GCC-specific BNPL service (as Tabby and Tamara successfully did, adapting to local credit landscapes and consumer behaviors) or even a next-generation payment solution that leapfrogs existing models by incorporating unique regional strengths, like advanced digital identity frameworks or Islamic finance principles. Thinking about my own project, I took inspiration from what they did. Klarna and PayPal are ideal for building for my startup - Krti. This reflective process is key.

PayPal (US-based Fintech): PayPal was a pioneer in online payments, making e-commerce transactions secure and straightforward. Studying PayPal's journey involves understanding how it built trust in a nascent online world, how it scaled its network of users and merchants, its strategies for international expansion, and its continuous innovation in areas like mobile payments and digital wallets. For a GCC founder, the lessons from PayPal could inspire ventures in cross-border e-commerce payments tailored to the Middle East and Africa, secure digital identity solutions, or platforms that facilitate SME financial management in the region, potentially expanding to other emerging markets. The core is to distill the principles of success—user trust, network effects, solving critical pain points—and apply them to new opportunities.

This methodology of deep study, adaptation, and innovation, drawing from global best practices while being acutely aware of local market dynamics, is a powerful approach for GCC founders aiming to build businesses that succeed regionally and have the potential for global impact. It's about standing on the shoulders of giants to see further and build better.

Building a globally competitive company, rooted in emerging technologies and launched from the GCC, is an ambitious endeavor. It requires more than just a brilliant idea or access to capital; it demands a specific set of conditions and, most importantly, a cultivated global mindset from day one. Start learning from other success stories and develop your own model of how you want your idea to be established and scale up.

This learning is the foundation, but several other conditions are critical:

Think Globally, Act Locally (Initially): While the ultimate ambition may be global, the initial product-market fit often needs to be achieved within a specific local or regional context. However, the product architecture, business model, and team culture should be designed with global scalability in mind from the outset. This means choosing technologies that scale, building processes that can be replicated, and fostering a company culture that embraces diversity and international perspectives.

World-Class Product and Talent: To compete on the global stage, your product or service must meet or exceed international standards of quality, user experience, and innovation. This necessitates a relentless focus on product excellence and the ability to attract, retain, and develop world-class talent. While the GCC talent pool is growing, founders must be prepared to recruit globally if necessary and invest heavily in training while creating an environment where top talent can thrive.

Deep Understanding of International Markets: Expanding globally requires more than just translating your website. It involves a deep understanding of different cultural nuances, regulatory environments, competitive landscapes, and consumer behaviors in each target market. This requires thorough market research, a willingness to adapt your offerings, and potentially establishing local teams or strategic partnerships.

Intellectual Property (IP) Strategy: For companies built on deeptech or significant technological innovation, a robust IP strategy is crucial. This involves not only creating novel IP but also actively protecting it through patents, trademarks, and other mechanisms in key international markets. This can be a significant source of competitive advantage and value creation.

Access to Global Networks and Capital: While the GCC offers significant funding opportunities, scaling globally often requires access to international venture capital, strategic partners, and global distribution networks. Founders should proactively build relationships with international investors and industry leaders, participate in global conferences, and seek mentorship from those who have successfully scaled businesses internationally.

Resilience and Adaptability: The journey of global expansion is fraught with challenges and uncertainties. Founders must possess immense resilience, the ability to learn from setbacks, and the adaptability to pivot their strategies in response to changing market conditions. What works in one region may not work in another, and the ability to iterate and evolve is paramount.

Cultivating these conditions and this global mindset within a GCC-based startup is the key to leveraging the region's strengths as a launchpad for companies that can not only lead in emerging trends but also make a significant impact on the world stage.

SUMMARY

Transformative Power of Emerging Technologies in the GCC

- **Emerging Trends**: Explored the significance of AI, robotics, fintech, healthtech, edtech, and deeptech as fundamental shifts creating opportunities for founders.
- **Key Takeaway**: Learn from the big guys. You can do it too if you open your mind and model your ideas.
- **Supportive Environment**: The GCC offers a strategic vision, investment capacity, and ambition to become a global innovation hub.
- **Path to Globalization**: The GCC can be a starting point for founders aiming to go global, leveraging emerging trends to drive innovation.
- **Call to Action**:
  - Envision future trends and open your mind to new ideas.
  - Actively participate in shaping technological change rather than observing it.
- **Identifying Opportunities**:
  - Seek unmet needs and disruption opportunities.
  - Aim for solutions that are significantly better (10×) rather than just incremental improvements.

- **Next Steps**:
  - ○ Sketch out bold ideas, conduct research, and network with experts.
  - ○ The GCC is ready to support ambitious founders who think big.
- **Your Journey Begins**: Start building a globally impactful Uni-Camel rooted in emerging trends now.

Additional Call to Action

- **Get Started Today**: Take the first step by identifying a specific technology trend that excites you. Research its applications in the GCC, connect with industry experts, and begin formulating your innovative solution. The time to act is now—don't wait for the right moment; create it.

Having explored the powerful emerging trends that are shaping our future and the immense potential to build globally impactful companies from the GCC, it becomes clear that such monumental ambitions demand more than just a great idea or access to cutting-edge technology. They require a specific, resilient, and highly evolved mindset.

How do you think about the future of the world?

This profound question leads us directly to the very core of entrepreneurial endurance and visionary leadership. Therefore, the next essential step in our journey will be to delve deeply into the mindset of a founder, revisiting and amplifying this critical theme specifically for the unique challenges and extraordinary opportunities presented by navigating the frontiers of global-scale innovation, and leading ventures at the shores of these emerging technological waves.

CHAPTER 7

GLOBAL UNICORN INSPIRATION

What You Can Learn from the World's Billion-Dollar Startups

Now, as we transition from the 'what'—the understanding of these future-shaping technologies—we delve into the 'who' and the 'how' at a more profound level.

It is not enough to merely identify a trend; one must possess the intrinsic qualities to capitalize on it, to navigate the turbulent waters of entrepreneurship, and to build an enterprise of enduring value. This chapter shifts our focus to the very essence of the founder. We will distill universal lessons from the journeys of globally recognized billion-dollar startups, applying these timeless principles to the specific context and opportunities within the GCC. Our central exploration will revolve around a critical, often underestimated, attribute: the founder's mindset.

DISCIPLINED DETERMINATION

In the vibrant yet challenging startup world, where gaps in the market can indeed become goldmines, the path is invariably strewn with doubts, fears, and unforeseen obstacles. The GCC, with its governments investing heavily in innovation and an ecosystem still young enough to offer less competition and more direct support, presents uniquely fertile ground. Yet, even in such a supportive environment, what truly separates the ventures that flourish into Uni-Camels from those that fizzle out? It isn't merely the brilliance of an idea or the size of the initial funding. Starting anything new will always demand a core strength from within you, a key skill that transcends all others. That indispensable quality, the bedrock of enduring entrepreneurial success, is **Disciplined Determination**.

This chapter will instill in you a deep understanding of the critical mindset that underpins the success of Uni-Camel founders worldwide, a mindset that, according to many experts, accounts for as much as 70% of their eventual triumph. You will learn about the key skills and intrinsic attributes that differentiate true entrepreneurs and visionary leaders from other professionals, with a laser focus on cultivating disciplined determination. While we acknowledge the continued relevance of top technological trends like AI, robotics, fintech, healthtech, and edtech as fertile grounds for opportunity—a recurring theme in our exploration—this chapter emphasizes the *founder* who navigates these trends.

CORE ATTRIBUTES OF A UNI-CAMEL FOUNDER

For any aspiring Uni-Camel founder, particularly one aiming to make their mark from the GCC, understanding and internalizing the global Uni-Camel mindset—especially the profound importance of disciplined determination—is not just beneficial; it is absolutely fundamental. Why is this so crucial? Because the entrepreneurial journey, irrespective of geographic advantages or market potential, is inherently a marathon, not a sprint. It is a relentless series of trials, tribulations, and, yes, triumphs. **Every time you try something new you fail—you learn, and you keep learning. They form building blocks to develop from there.** This is the unvarnished truth of innovation.

Taking failure not as a full stop but as an **adventure** in learning, navigating persistent **uncertainty**, and understanding that **some startups fail multiple times but they do succeed eventually** requires a deep well of inner strength. The GCC's supportive ecosystem, with its governmental backing and burgeoning investment landscape, can undoubtedly accelerate growth and mitigate certain external pressures. However, it cannot insulate a founder from the internal battles of self-doubt, the exhaustion of relentless effort, or the sting of rejection. It is the **spirit of eagerness and determination**, the unwavering **discipline** to persist when things get tough, that sustains founders through these inevitable challenges. This journey demands **sacrifices: you will have to put**

your time and energy. It is **not a typical day job**. It is a consuming passion where **you eat**, **sleep and live your startup dream**. Therefore, learning to cultivate this resilient, disciplined, and determined mindset is paramount. It is the internal compass and engine that will guide you through the storms and ultimately determine your capacity for long-term survival, growth, and the extraordinary success you envision.

THE PILLARS OF A UNI-CAMEL FOUNDER MINDSET

The journey to Uni-Camel status is less about a single stroke of genius and more about the consistent application of a specific set of mental and behavioral attributes. While the startup world often glorifies the visionary idea, it is the founder's underlying mindset that truly forges billion-dollar enterprises from the raw material of innovation.

Startup is not for everyone: You will face barriers like procrastination and excuses. Overcoming these internal and external hurdles requires more than just intelligence or creativity; it demands a robust psychological framework. **This kind of lifestyle is not easy, but it is possible for everyone to do it**: provided **you are determined and committed to bring change in people's lives**, **it can be done**. Let's dissect the core pillars of this Uni-Camel founder mindset, drawing inspiration from global successes and tailoring it to the GCC context.

a. Vision: Seeing Beyond the Horizon

Vision, in the context of a Uni-Camel founder, transcends merely having a good idea. It is the ability to see a future state that others may not yet perceive, to articulate that future with compelling clarity, and to inspire a team, investors, and customers to believe in and work towards that distant horizon. Global unicorn founders, from Steve Jobs at Apple with his vision for democratizing computing and creating insanely great products, to Elon Musk with his audacious goals for sustainable energy and interplanetary travel, have all been driven by powerful, often contrarian, visions. This isn't just about predicting the future; it's about actively shaping it. For a GCC founder, this means looking beyond immediate market needs to anticipate how regional and global dynamics will evolve. It involves envisioning how their venture can not only solve a local problem but also scale to address broader challenges or opportunities, potentially positioning the GCC as a leader in a specific niche. A strong vision provides the guiding star during periods of uncertainty and serves as the ultimate motivator for the entire organization.

b. Disciplined Determination (the Core Theme): The Unwavering Engine of Success

This is the linchpin, the attribute that the blueprint correctly identifies as the great differentiator. Disciplined determination is an amalgam of unwavering focus, profound resilience in the face of setbacks, and an unshakeable commitment to long-term goals, even when short-term realities are painful or discouraging. It's the capacity to consistently push through the barriers of procrastination, self-doubt, and external criticism. Think of Jeff Bezos' relentless, decades-long focus on customer obsession and long-term growth for Amazon, often in the face of investor skepticism about profitability. Or consider the sheer tenacity of countless founders who pivoted multiple times, faced near-bankruptcy, or endured years of struggle before achieving breakthrough success. In the GCC context, while the support systems are growing, founders will still encounter bureaucratic hurdles, market education challenges, and competitive pressures. Disciplined determination means not giving up when the first, second, or even tenth attempt doesn't yield the desired results. It means meticulously planning, executing with focus, learning from every outcome, and relentlessly pursuing the vision with a disciplined approach to daily actions and strategic objectives. It is the quiet, persistent engine that drives a startup through the inevitable storms towards its ultimate destination.

c. Eagerness to Learn (Continuous Learning & Adaptability): Embracing Evolution

The startup landscape is in a perpetual state of flux. Technologies evolve, market preferences shift, and new competitors emerge. Founders who believe they have all the answers are quickly left behind. A hallmark of successful global unicorn leaders is their insatiable **eagerness to learn**. This involves embracing failure not as a personal defeat but as an invaluable learning opportunity. It means actively seeking out new knowledge, challenging one's own assumptions, and being willing to adapt strategies based on new information and market feedback. Satya Nadella's transformation of

Microsoft, fostering a culture of learning and empathy, is a powerful example. For GCC founders, this is particularly crucial. As a dynamic and rapidly evolving market, the ability to learn quickly—from local customer behavior, from global best practices, from technological advancements—and adapt business models accordingly is paramount. This continuous learning mindset ensures that the venture remains agile, relevant, and capable of seizing new opportunities as they arise.

d. Ability to Face Rejection (Thick-skinned Resilience): The Armor of the Entrepreneur

The entrepreneurial path is paved with rejection. Investors will say no, potential customers will choose competitors, product launches might be met with indifference, and critics will voice their doubts. A founder who internalizes every rejection or negative feedback will quickly become demoralized and paralyzed. Developing a **thick skin**, an ability to face rejection with resilience, is essential. This doesn't mean ignoring feedback; it means developing the capacity to process it objectively, extract any valuable lessons, and continue moving forward without letting it erode one's core belief in the vision. Many globally successful founders have shared stories of countless rejections before securing their first major investment or customer. In the GCC, while the ecosystem is supportive, founders will still need to pitch to numerous investors, convince skeptical partners, and win over customers. The ability to bounce back from these rejections, learn from them, and refine one's approach is a critical survival skill.

e. Communication and Team Leadership: Inspiring Collective Action

A founder cannot build a Uni-Camel alone. The ability to articulate the vision in a compelling way, to motivate and inspire a diverse team, and to build a strong, cohesive company culture is indispensable. Effective communication is not just about eloquent speeches; it's about clarity, transparency, active listening, and the ability to rally people around a shared purpose. Leaders like Howard Schultz of Starbucks built a global empire not just on coffee, but on a culture that valued its employees. For GCC founders, this means being able to attract and retain top talent (both local and international), fostering an environment of collaboration and innovation, and effectively communicating the company's mission and values to all stakeholders. As the venture scales, the founder's role increasingly becomes about leading and empowering others, making strong communication and team leadership skills non-negotiable.

These pillars—Vision, Disciplined Determination, Eagerness to Learn, Resilience to Rejection, and Communication/Team Leadership—are not innate traits possessed by a select few. They are skills and mindset attributes that can be consciously cultivated and strengthened over time. For the GCC founder aspiring to global Uni-Camel status, mastering these is the key to unlocking their full potential and navigating the exhilarating, demanding journey ahead.

ACTIONABLE INSIGHTS & GCC RELEVANCE

Cultivating the Uni-Camel founder mindset is an active, ongoing process. It's not enough to simply understand these pillars; aspiring founders must actively work to embody them. This section provides actionable insights and reiterates why the GCC is a particularly relevant arena for this mindset to flourish.

Action Point: Taking the Right Steps – One at a Time

You're in the right place at the right time. Now it's about taking the right steps—one at a time. This emphasizes that grand ambitions are realized through consistent, incremental progress. To start cultivating the Uni-Camel mindset, consider these actionable steps:

1. Set Micro-Goals for Disciplined Determination: Break down your large vision into smaller, manageable daily or weekly goals. Achieving these consistently builds momentum and reinforces the habit of discipline. Track your progress and hold yourself accountable.

2. Actively Seek Mentorship & Feedback: Identify experienced entrepreneurs or industry leaders (both globally and within the GCC) who embody the traits you admire. Seek their mentorship. More importantly, actively solicit honest feedback on your ideas and your approach, and practice receiving it with an open, learning-oriented attitude, even if it's critical. This builds resilience and accelerates learning.

3. Practice Resilience Through Deliberate Challenges: Step outside your comfort zone regularly. Take on tasks or projects that stretch your abilities and where failure is a possibility. Each time you navigate a setback and learn from it, you strengthen your resilience muscle. This could be anything from public speaking to tackling a complex technical problem.

4. Journal for Self-Reflection and Vision Clarity: Dedicate time for regular self-reflection. Journaling can help clarify your vision, track your learning, process failures, and reinforce your commitment. It's a powerful tool for maintaining focus and an '**eagerness to learn.**'

5. Build Your Communication Muscle: Practice articulating your vision and ideas clearly and persuasively in different settings—to potential co-founders, mentors, or even friends and family. Join networking groups or public speaking clubs to hone these skills.

REITERATION OF GCC ADVANTAGES: THE FERTILE GROUND FOR A POWERFUL MINDSET

My View on the Uni-Camel and Its Future in the GCC: Why the GCC is positioned for billion-dollar outcomes

The GCC's unique characteristics—its less saturated markets in many tech verticals, strong governmental backing for innovation, significant capital availability, and a young, tech-savvy population—create an environment where a founder with the right mindset can achieve accelerated growth. These external supportive factors, as discussed in the earlier chapter, mean that a founder's disciplined determination and vision are more likely to yield tangible results, creating positive feedback loops that further strengthen their resolve. The **gaps become gold** more readily when the ecosystem is actively encouraging and enabling new ventures.

Mindset as the Foundation of Authority

The concept of **establishing authority in your industry is in reference to how to define your voice and be seen as a thought leader**. This is intrinsically linked to the founder's mindset. True thought leadership doesn't come from merely proclaiming expertise; it stems from a deep-seated vision, a commitment to continuous learning, the ability to communicate complex ideas clearly (all pillars of the founder mindset), and a genuine desire to add value to one's industry. Founders who embody disciplined determination in their pursuit of knowledge and innovation naturally begin to establish authority. Their consistent efforts, their willingness to share insights (even from failures), and their clear articulation of a forward-looking vision position them as leaders others want to follow and learn from.

Adapting Global Frameworks: The Intelligent Application of a Learning Mindset

GCC entrepreneurs can learn much from adapting international frameworks to local realities. This is where the 'eagerness to learn' and 'vision' pillars of the mindset truly shine. It's not about blindly copying what worked elsewhere.

It's about having the intellectual curiosity to study global successes deeply, the analytical skill to distill the underlying principles, and the creative vision to adapt those principles innovatively to the specific cultural, economic, and regulatory context of the GCC. This intelligent adaptation, driven by a robust learning mindset, is what allows founders to leverage global knowledge to create uniquely successful regional, and eventually global, enterprises.

THE NON-NEGOTIABLES OF THE UNI-CAMEL QUEST

While the journey of every Uni-Camel founder is unique, certain internal conditions, inspired by the tenacity of global trailblazers, are non-negotiable. These are the bedrock attributes that a founder must possess or relentlessly cultivate to even have a chance at achieving billion-dollar scale and impact.

First and foremost is an **unwavering commitment** that transcends mere interest or enthusiasm. This is a deep, almost visceral dedication to the problem being solved and the vision for the company. It's the fuel that keeps a founder going when initial excitement wanes, when challenges mount, and when the path ahead is shrouded in uncertainty. This commitment must be coupled with a **willingness to make profound sacrifices**. This often means sacrificing personal time, financial stability in the short term, and sometimes even relationships, all in pursuit of the larger vision. It's a level of dedication that borders on obsession, but an obsession channeled productively through disciplined action.

Another non-negotiable is a **deep-seated**, **almost unshakeable belief in their vision**, even when faced with widespread skepticism or repeated setbacks. This isn't blind faith, but a conviction rooted in deep market understanding, customer empathy, and a clear sight of the future they are trying to create. This belief acts as an internal gyroscope, keeping the founder steady amidst external turbulence.

Finally, there must be a **relentless pursuit of excellence** in every aspect of the venture—from product development and customer service to team building and strategic execution. Mediocrity is the enemy of Uni-Camel ambitions. This pursuit of excellence is not about perfectionism, which can lead to paralysis, but about a constant striving to be better, to learn faster, and to deliver exceptional value. **Opportunity is everywhere. Startups succeed by seeing a gap before others and moving quickly,** It is this combination of unwavering commitment, willingness to sacrifice, profound belief, and relentless pursuit of excellence, all supercharged by disciplined determination, that forms the internal crucible from which Uni-Camels are forged.

SUMMARY

Global Unicorn Inspiration and Founder's Mindset

- **Essence of the Uni-Camel Founder's Mindset**:
  - ◦ **Disciplined Determination** – Central quality for transforming visionary ideas into valuable enterprises.

- Internal attributes, shaped by global best practices and entrepreneurial challenges, dictate success.
- **GCC Advantages**:
  - The region offers a fertile ground for innovation and growth.
  - Success ultimately relies on the founder's mindset and internal qualities.
- **Challenges of the Journey**:
  - The path demands sacrifice, continuous learning, and the ability to navigate uncertainty and rejection.
  - Cultivating an indomitable spirit leads to profound rewards and the potential for meaningful change.

Call to Action: Forge Your Founder's Mindset

- **Active Engagement**: The insights from billion-dollar startups are a call to action, not for passive consumption.
- **Self-Assessment**:
  - Evaluate your mindset against key pillars:
    - Clear and compelling Vision
    - Unwavering Disciplined Determination
    - Eagerness to Learn and Adapt
    - Resilience to Face Rejection
    - Communication and Team Leadership skills.
- **Commitment to Growth**:
  - Focus on continuous cultivation of these traits as a lifelong practice.
  - Start today by seeking challenges, embracing feedback, and dedicating time to learning and reflection.
- **Mentorship**: Find mentors who exemplify these qualities to guide your development.

- **Interconnected Growth**: Recognize that your personal growth as a founder is closely linked to your startup's success. Embark on self-development with the same passion you have for your business idea.

A FINAL WORD — THE UNI-CAMEL JOURNEY AWAITS

Throughout this book, we have journeyed from understanding the foundational mindset of a Uni-Camel founder to exploring the unique potential of the GCC, dissecting local success stories, navigating emerging global trends, and finally, returning to the core essence of the entrepreneurial spirit. The path to building a billion-dollar startup is complex and demanding, yet, as we have seen, it is achievable, particularly within a supportive and ambitious ecosystem like the GCC.

The future of entrepreneurship in this region, and indeed globally, will be shaped by founders like you—those who dare to dream big, who are willing to embrace the unknown, and who execute their visions with unwavering, disciplined determination. The opportunities are immense, the support systems are strengthening, and the world is eager for innovative solutions. The Uni-Camel journey awaits. Embrace it with courage, wisdom, and the indomitable spirit we have explored. Your potential to create something truly transformative is limited only by the scope of your vision and the depth of your determination.

PART 3

The Uni-Camel Founder Philosophy

This part provides a comprehensive roadmap for founders looking to efficiently turn their vision into a viable product. By simplifying product concepts, utilizing design sprints to create prototypes, and implementing effective go-to-market strategies, entrepreneurs can navigate the early stages of market entry successfully. Each chapter equips founders with practical tools and insights to build fast and effectively launch their MVPs.

CHAPTER 8

THE MIND OF A GCC FOUNDER

The Psychological Backbone of Billion-Dollar Ambition

WHAT SEPARATES FOUNDERS FROM DREAMERS

There's a moment when ambition transforms into something else. It stops being a wish. It stops being a fantasy. It becomes a *force*.

I've worked with hundreds of entrepreneurs in the GCC. Some have gone on to build billion-dollar companies. Others have built interesting startups that plateau. Still others have faded away.

The difference isn't intelligence. It's not access to capital. It's not even the quality of the initial idea.

The difference is psychological. It's how they think about themselves. It's how they think about their role. It's how they navigate uncertainty. It's how they maintain discipline when no one is watching. It's how they balance confidence with humility. It's how they see themselves as a force, not just someone playing a role.

This is the mind of a GCC founder. This is the psychological backbone separating those who build billion-dollar companies from those who don't.

AMBITION AND OWNERSHIP: THE FOUNDATION

Let me start with something that sounds simple but is profoundly rare: true ownership.

Most people are employees. They work for someone else. They execute someone else's vision. They're compensated for their time and effort. This is a valid choice…but it's not the founder's choice.

A founder owns something. They own the outcome. They own the risk. They own the vision. They own the responsibility.

This ownership is not a legal construct. You can be a founder without owning equity. You can own equity without being a founder. The ownership I'm talking about is psychological ownership.

It's the mindset that says: 'This is mine. Its success is my success. Its failure is my failure. I am responsible for its outcome.'

This psychological ownership changes everything. It changes how you make decisions. It changes how you respond to setbacks. It changes how you treat your team. It changes how you navigate uncertainty.

THE OWNERSHIP PARADOX

Here's what's interesting: the founders who build billion-dollar companies are the ones who have the deepest sense of ownership, but the least attachment to being right.

They own the outcome, but they're willing to change their approach if the market tells them they're wrong. They own the vision, but they're willing to adapt the vision if circumstances change. They own the responsibility, but they're willing to delegate and trust their team.

This is the ownership paradox. It's the ability to be deeply committed to something while remaining flexible about how you achieve it.

OWNERSHIP IN THE GCC CONTEXT

In the GCC, ownership has a particular weight. In a region where relationships and reputation matter, ownership means something deeper than just legal responsibility.

When you own a company in the GCC, you're not just responsible for financial outcomes. You're responsible for your reputation, how you treat people, and maintaining trust. Also, you're responsible for contributing to the region's transformation.

This deeper sense of ownership is what separates founders who build enduring companies from those who build companies designed for a quick exit.

DISCIPLINE AS IDENTITY: THE UNGLAMOROUS FOUNDATION

Want to know what separates founders who succeed from those who fail? Don't look at their intelligence, their charisma, or their network. Instead, look at their discipline.

But not the kind of discipline that's forced from outside. The kind of discipline that's built into your identity. The kind where discipline isn't something you do—it's who you are.

What Discipline Means

Discipline is:

- Doing what you said you would do, even when it's inconvenient

- Maintaining your standards, even when no one is watching
- Making the hard choice, not the easy choice
- Staying focused, even when shiny new opportunities distract you
- Showing up, even when you don't feel like it
- Finishing what you start, even when it's difficult
- Learning from mistakes, not making excuses.

Discipline is not about being inflexible. Instead, it's about having a system that allows you to execute consistently, even when conditions are difficult.

Discipline as a Competitive Advantage

In the GCC, discipline is a competitive advantage. Why? Because the region moves fast. Opportunities emerge and disappear quickly. Capital flows rapidly. Regulations change. Market conditions shift.

In this environment, the founders who win are the ones who have built discipline into their identity. They have systems, routines, and processes. They have the ability to execute consistently, even when everything around them is changing.

By contrast, the founders who lack discipline get distracted. They chase every shiny opportunity, starting multiple projects without finishing any of them. They make promises they don't keep. They lose focus. They lose momentum. In short, they *lose*.

The Discipline Paradox

Here's something interesting: The most successful founders are the ones who have built discipline into their identity, but who are also willing to break their own rules when the situation demands it.

They have systems, But they're not slaves to their systems. They have routines, But they're willing to abandon them when circumstances change. They have processes. But they're willing to take shortcuts when speed is critical.

This is the discipline paradox. It's the ability to be disciplined and flexible at the same time.

BUILDING DISCIPLINE AS IDENTITY

How do you build discipline as identity? It's not something that happens overnight. Instead, it's built through small, consistent choices.

- **Start small**: Don't try to overhaul your entire life—start with one thing and commit to doing it consistently.
- **Make it visible**: Tell people about your commitment. Make it public, which creates accountability.
- **Track it**: Measure your progress, because seeing yourself getting better reinforces the identity.
- **Celebrate it**: When you follow through, acknowledge and let yourself feel good about it.
- **Extend it**: Once you've built discipline in one area, extend it to other areas.

Over time, discipline stops being something you do and becomes who you are. And when it's your identity, you don't have to think about it. You just do it.

CONFIDENCE VS. HUMILITY: THE FOUNDER'S PARADOX

One of the most misunderstood aspects of founder psychology is the relationship between confidence and humility.

Many people think these are opposites. They think a confident founder is arrogant, while a humble founder is insecure.

But the founders who build billion-dollar companies are the ones who have mastered both. They have 'confident humility'.

What Confident Humility Means

Confident humility is:
- Believing in your vision while remaining open to being wrong
- Trusting your judgment while seeking input from others
- Being decisive while remaining curious
- Knowing your strengths while acknowledging your weaknesses
- Taking responsibility while learning from others
- Pushing forward while listening to feedback.

It's the ability to be strong and open at the same time. To be sure of yourself and uncertain at the same time. To be a leader and a learner at the same time.

Why This Matters in the GCC

Confident humility is particularly important in the GCC, because the region values both strength and respect.

Founders who are purely confident—those who are arrogant, don't listen, and think they have all the answers—lose respect. They lose relationships, as well as the trust that's essential for success in the region.

Founders who are purely humble—who are insecure, who second-guess themselves, who can't make decisions—lose credibility, momentum, and the ability to inspire their team and their investors.

The founders who succeed are the ones who have confident humility. They're strong enough to make decisions and take risks, while being humble enough to listen, to learn, and to adapt.

Building Confident Humility

How do you build confident humility? It starts with understanding that confidence and humility aren't opposites, but complements.

- **Know your strengths**: Understand what you're good at, then build on those strengths. This builds confidence.
- **Know your weaknesses**: Understand what you're not good at, then acknowledge these weaknesses. This builds humility.

- **Seek input**: Ask for advice. Listen to feedback. Learn from others. This builds humility.
- **Make decisions**: Don't get paralyzed by seeking input. You have to decide at some point, which builds confidence.
- **Admit mistakes**: When you're wrong, say so. Learn from your mistake, as this builds humility.
- **Stand by your vision**: When you believe in something, fight for it. This builds confidence.

Over time, you develop the ability to be both confident and humble, strong and open, a leader and a learner.

NAVIGATING UNCERTAINTY: THE GCC FOUNDER'S UNIQUE CHALLENGE

Uncertainty is part of any founder's journey, but the uncertainty in the GCC is unique.

In Silicon Valley, the uncertainty is primarily about product-market fit and capital. Will customers want this product? Will I be able to raise capital?

In the GCC, the uncertainty is broader. It includes product-market fit and capital, but it also includes regulatory uncertainty, political uncertainty, capital flow uncertainty, and market uncertainty.

Types of Uncertainty in the GCC

Regulatory Uncertainty: As the regulatory environment evolves, what's allowed today might not be allowed tomorrow. What's prohibited today might be encouraged tomorrow.

You have to navigate this uncertainty while building your business.

Political Uncertainty: Political dynamics in the region can shift. Government priorities can change. What was a priority last year might not be a priority this year. You have to navigate this uncertainty while building relationships with government.

Capital Flow Uncertainty: Capital in the GCC flows based on oil prices, government priorities, and global market conditions. Because capital that's abundant one year might be scarce the next, you have to navigate this uncertainty while planning your growth.

Market Uncertainty: The GCC market is still developing. Customer preferences are evolving, competitive dynamics are changing, and market conditions can shift rapidly. You have to navigate this uncertainty while building your product.

How GCC Founders Navigate Uncertainty

The founders who succeed in the GCC are the ones who have developed specific capabilities for navigating uncertainty:

1. Scenario Planning

Successful GCC founders spend time thinking about what could go wrong. What if regulations change? What if capital flows shift? What if a competitor enters the market? What if a political shift changes the landscape?

By thinking through scenarios, they're better prepared when uncertainty becomes reality. They're not caught off guard, as they have contingency plans. Flexibility is built into their business model.

2. Relationship Building
In an uncertain environment, relationships are your anchor. When you have strong relationships with regulators, partners, customers, and investors, you have people you can turn to when uncertainty emerges.

These relationships provide information. They provide guidance. They provide support. They provide opportunities. In an uncertain environment, relationships are your most valuable asset.

3. Financial Resilience
Instead of spending every dollar they make, successful GCC founders build financial reserves that allow them to weather uncertainty.

When uncertainty emerges—when capital flows shift, market conditions change, or unexpected challenges arise—companies with financial resilience can adapt, but companies without financial resilience struggle.

4. Speed of Adaptation
When uncertainty becomes reality, the founders who adapt quickly survive. This means having decision-making processes that allow for rapid adaptation. It means having a

culture that embraces change. It means having leaders who can make decisions under conditions of uncertainty.

5. Clarity of Purpose

In an uncertain environment, clarity of purpose is your compass. When you're clear about what problem you're solving and why it matters, you can navigate uncertainty without losing direction.

You might change your approach. You might adapt your strategy, but you maintain clarity about your core mission. This clarity allows you to make decisions even when you don't have perfect information.

THE FOUNDER AS A FORCE: NOT A ROLE, BUT AN IDENTITY

Here's something that separates founders who build billion-dollar companies from those who don't: they see themselves as a force, not as someone playing a role.

What's the difference?

A role is something you do. You're a CEO. You're an entrepreneur. You're a founder. It's a title. It's a job description.

A force is something you are. You're someone who moves things. You're someone who shapes outcomes. You're someone who influences the ecosystem around you. You're someone who creates momentum.

The Founder as a Force

When you see yourself as a force, everything changes.

You don't wait for permission. You don't ask for approval. You don't hope things work out. You make things happen.

You understand that your energy, your vision, your discipline, your confidence, your humility—all of these things ripple out into the world. They influence your team. They influence your investors. They influence your customers. They influence the market.

You're not just building a company. You're shaping an ecosystem. You're creating momentum. You're creating a force.

The Responsibility of Being a Force

But being a force comes with responsibility. Your energy can inspire or demoralize. Your vision can unite or divide. Your discipline can motivate or intimidate. Your confidence can build trust or create arrogance.

The founders who build billion-dollar companies are the ones who understand this responsibility. They understand that they're not just building a company. They're shaping an ecosystem. They're influencing people. They're creating a force.

And they take this responsibility seriously.

Building Your Force

How do you build yourself into a force? It starts with the elements we've already discussed:

- **Ownership**: Take full responsibility for your outcomes
- **Discipline**: Build systems that allow you to execute consistently
- **Confident Humility**: Be strong and open at the same time
- **Navigate Uncertainty**: Build relationships, plan scenarios, maintain resilience
- **Clarity of Purpose**: Be clear about what you're building and why.

When you combine these elements, you become a force. You become someone who shapes outcomes. You become someone who creates momentum. You become someone who influences the ecosystem around you.

And when you're a force, you attract people who want to be part of what you're building. You attract investors who want to fund you. You attract customers who want to use your product. You attract partners who want to work with you.

You become someone who builds billion-dollar companies.

THE GCC FOUNDER'S PSYCHOLOGICAL ADVANTAGE

Here's something important: As a GCC founder, you have a psychological advantage that founders in other regions don't have.

In the GCC, you're building in a region that's hungry for success stories. You're building in a region where entrepreneurship is celebrated. You're building in a region where government is actively supporting innovation.

This creates a psychological advantage. You're not fighting against the system. You're not fighting against cultural headwinds. You're building with the wind at your back.

But this advantage can also be a trap. It can make you complacent. It can make you think that success is inevitable. It can make you lazy.

The founders who win are the ones who understand this advantage but don't rely on it. They work as hard as founders in other regions. They maintain the same discipline. They navigate the same uncertainties. But they do it with the advantage of building in a region that wants them to succeed.

THE PSYCHOLOGICAL FOUNDATION
The mind of a GCC founder is built on:
- **Ownership**: Taking full responsibility for your outcomes
- **Discipline**: Building systems that allow you to execute consistently
- **Confident Humility**: Being strong and open at the same time
- **Navigating Uncertainty**: Building relationships, planning scenarios, maintaining resilience
- **Clarity of Purpose**: Being clear about what you're building and why

- **Seeing Yourself as a Force**: Understanding that you shape outcomes and influence ecosystems.

These are the psychological foundations of billion-dollar ambition in the GCC.

They're not something you're born with. They're built through consistent choices, through deliberate practice, through learning from mistakes, through staying committed to your vision even when it's difficult.

But when you build these foundations, you become someone who can build a billion-dollar company. You become a founder. You become a force.

SUMMARY

The Mind of a GCC Founder: Psychological Backbone

Ambition and Ownership
- True ownership is psychological, not just legal
- Own the outcome, own the risk, own the vision
- The ownership paradox: deeply committed but flexible about approach
- In the GCC, ownership includes reputation and contribution.

Discipline as Identity
- Discipline is doing what you said you would do, consistently
- Built through small, consistent choices
- Becomes who you are, not just what you do
- Competitive advantage in a fast-moving market.

Confident Humility
- Believe in your vision while remaining open to being wrong
- Trust your judgment while seeking input
- Be decisive while remaining curious
- Particularly important in the GCC's relationship-driven culture.

Navigating Uncertainty
- Regulatory, political, capital flow, and market uncertainty
- Navigate through scenario planning, relationship building, financial resilience, speed of adaptation, clarity of purpose
- Relationships are your anchor in uncertainty
- Financial reserves allow you to weather change.

The Founder as a Force
- Not a role, but an identity
- You shape outcomes and influence ecosystems
- Your energy, vision, discipline ripple out into the world
- Comes with the responsibility to use this influence wisely.

The GCC Founder's Psychological Advantage
- Building in a region that wants you to succeed
- The wind at your back, but don't rely on it
- Work with the same discipline as founders in other regions
- Advantage: supportive ecosystem; Trap: complacency.

The Psychological Foundation
- Ownership
- Discipline
- Confident humility
- Navigation of uncertainty
- Clarity of purpose
- Seeing yourself as a force.

These foundations are built through consistent choices and deliberate practice. When you build them, you become someone who builds billion-dollar companies.

CHAPTER 9

MENTAL MODELS FOR CROSSING THE DESERT

The Thinking Tools of Billion-Dollar Founders

THE DIFFERENCE BETWEEN THINKING AND KNOWING

There's a difference between knowing something and having a mental model for it.

You can know that 'relationships matter in the GCC.' But if you have a mental model for how relationships compound over time, how trust creates gravitational pull, how reputation shapes outcomes—then you think differently. You make different decisions. You prioritize differently.

Mental models are the thinking tools separating founders who build billion-dollar companies from those who don't.

In this chapter, I'm sharing the mental models that have shaped my own thinking, along with the thinking of the most successful founders I know in the GCC. These aren't theories—they're frameworks drawn from real experience, tested in real markets, proven through real outcomes.

These are the thinking tools that will guide you from MVP to billion-dollar scale.

MENTAL MODEL 1: THE DESERT MODEL — ENDURANCE BEFORE SCALE

There's a fundamental difference between how entrepreneurs think in Silicon Valley and how they think in the GCC.

In Silicon Valley, the mindset is: 'Move fast and break things. Fail fast. Iterate rapidly. Get to scale as quickly as possible.'

In the GCC, the mindset is different. It's rooted in something deeper—something that comes from the region's history, its culture, its geography.

It's the Desert Model.

What the Desert Model Teaches

In the desert, survival comes first. You don't move fast and break things. You move deliberately and carefully. You understand your environment. You prepare for scarcity. You build resilience. You survive long enough to reach the oasis. And once you reach the oasis, you dominate it.

This isn't just philosophy. This is how the most successful companies in the GCC have been built.

Aramco's Desert Model

Saudi Aramco didn't become one of the world's most valuable companies by moving fast and breaking things. They became dominant by surviving long enough in the Saudi desert to understand the landscape, build relationships with the government, develop unmatched expertise, and then dominate their their market for over 80 years.

Aramco understood that in the GCC, long-term relationships matter more than short-term disruption. They understood that government relationships are essential. They understood that operational excellence and reliability are competitive advantages. They survived long enough to build a moat that competitors couldn't cross.

Careem's Desert Model

Careem didn't try to be Uber. They understood that the GCC market required a different approach. They moved carefully. They built relationships with regulators. They understood local preferences. They adapted their product to local needs. They survived long enough in each market to understand it deeply. And then they dominated.

When Uber entered the GCC market with a global playbook, they struggled. Careem, operating from the Desert Model, thrived. Careem understood that in the GCC, you don't move fast and break things. You move deliberately and build trust.

The Desert Model in Practice

What does the Desert Model mean for your company?

1. Survival comes before dominance: You can't dominate if you haven't survived. Build a sustainable business first. Scale comes later.

2. Relationships are infrastructure: In the desert, your relationships with other travelers, with guides, with oasis-keepers determine whether you survive. In the GCC business landscape, your relationships with regulators, partners, customers, and investors determine whether you survive.

3. Preparation matters: In the desert, you prepare carefully before you travel. You know where the water is. You know the route. You know the dangers. In business, preparation means understanding your market, understanding your customers, understanding the regulatory landscape.

4. Resilience is built into your DNA: Desert travelers don't panic when they face challenges. They adapt. They persist. They find alternative routes. Successful GCC founders have this same resilience built into their DNA.

5. Once you dominate, you *stay* dominant: The oasis is the most valuable place in the desert—so once you reach it and establish dominance, you protect it fiercely. Successful GCC companies don't move on to the next market until they've fully dominated their current market.

THE DESERT MODEL VS. THE SILICON VALLEY MODEL

Desert Model	Silicon Valley Model
Move fast and break things	Move deliberately and build trust
Fail fast	Learn fast (but maintain reputation)
Growth at all costs	Sustainable growth
Disrupt the market	Understand the market
Scale first, optimize later	Optimize first, scale later

The Desert Model isn't slower. It's smarter. It's adapted to the GCC market. It's how you build companies that last.

MENTAL MODEL 2: THE TRUST ENGINE — REPUTATION COMPOUNDS FASTER THAN CAPITAL

In Silicon Valley, the most valuable asset is capital. Founders obsess over raising capital. Investors obsess over deploying capital, which the ecosystem is built around.

In the GCC, the most valuable asset is trust.

This is the Trust Engine.

How the Trust Engine Works

The Trust Engine operates on a simple principle: your reputation precedes you.

When you walk into a room in the GCC, people already know something about you. They've heard about you from others. They know whether you're someone who keeps their word. They know whether you treat people well. They know whether you're trustworthy.

This reputation shapes how people interact with you. If you have a reputation for trust and integrity, doors open. If you have a reputation for cutting corners or treating people poorly, doors close.

Why Reputation Compounds Faster Than Capital

Capital is fungible. It's interchangeable. If you spend $1 million, it's gone. You have to raise more capital.

Reputation is different. It compounds. When you build trust with one person, that person tells others. Your reputation spreads. People want to work with you. Customers seek you out. Partners want to partner with you. Investors want to fund you. Talent wants to join you.

This gravitational pull is more powerful than any amount of capital. It's more valuable than any amount of marketing. It's the foundation of sustainable success in the GCC.

Building Your Trust Engine

Building a strong Trust Engine requires consistency over time. It requires:

1. **Doing what you say you're going to do**: This sounds simple, but it's rare. Most people over-promise and under-deliver. If you consistently do what you say you're going to do, you build a reputation for reliability.

2. **Treating people well, even when it's inconvenient**: In the GCC, how you treat people matters. If you treat people well when it's easy and poorly when it's difficult, people notice. If you treat people well consistently, you build a reputation for integrity.

3. **Being transparent about challenges**: When things go wrong, transparent communication builds trust. When you hide problems or make excuses, trust erodes. The founders who build strong Trust Engines are the ones who communicate honestly about challenges.

4. **Investing in relationships before you need them**: The best time to build a relationship with a regulator is before you need regulatory approval. The best time to build a relationship with a potential partner is before you need their partnership. The best time to build a relationship with an investor is before you need their capital.

5. **Maintaining your values even when it's costly**: The founders who build the strongest Trust Engines are the ones who maintain their values even when it would be more profitable to compromise. This consistency builds deep trust.

The Trust Engine as Competitive Advantage

In the GCC, a strong Trust Engine is your most defensible competitive advantage. Competitors can copy your product. They can copy your technology. They can copy your business model. But they can't copy your reputation.

When you have a reputation for trust and integrity, you can:
- Attract the best talent without offering the highest salaries
- Build partnerships that competitors can't access
- Navigate regulatory challenges more smoothly
- Raise capital more easily
- Retain customers more effectively
- Weather crises more successfully.

The founders who build billion-dollar companies in the GCC are the ones who understand that their reputation is their most valuable asset. They protect it fiercely. They build it consistently. They let it guide their decisions.

MENTAL MODEL 3: THE SANDSTORM PRINCIPLE — ADAPTATION BEATS SPEED

One of the most powerful mental models that separates billion-dollar founders is their ability to see challenges not as obstacles, but as opportunities to adapt.

This is the Sandstorm Principle.

What the Sandstorm Principle Teaches

A sandstorm in the desert is sudden and powerful. It changes the landscape. It obscures vision. It forces you to adapt quickly or be buried. Successful desert travelers don't panic when a sandstorm hits. They adapt. They find shelter. They wait it out. They continue their journey.

Successful GCC founders operate the same way. They understand that sandstorms—sudden market changes, regulatory shifts, political dynamics, capital flow changes— are part of the landscape. They don't panic. They adapt. They find shelter. They wait it out. They continue their journey.

Examples of Sandstorms in the GCC

The GCC market has experienced multiple sandstorms:

- **The Oil Price Collapse (2014–2016)**
When oil prices collapsed, capital flows changed dramatically. Government spending decreased. Investment priorities shifted. Companies that had been growing rapidly suddenly faced capital constraints. Companies that had built sustainable business models survived and thrived, while those that had been dependent on cheap capital struggled.

The founders who adapted quickly—who shifted their business models, reduced costs, and found new sources of capital—survived and thrived. By contrast, the founders who didn't adapt quickly struggled.

- **The Regulatory Evolution in Fintech**

When fintech companies started operating in the GCC, the regulatory environment was unclear. Companies experimented. Some pushed boundaries, while others worked closely with regulators. As the regulatory environment evolved, companies that had built strong relationships with regulators and had been transparent about their operations thrived. Companies that had tried to operate in gray areas struggled.

- **The COVID-19 Pandemic**

When COVID-19 hit, the GCC market experienced a sudden shock. Companies that had been dependent on physical presence struggled. Companies that had adapted quickly to digital-first models thrived. Companies that had built resilient supply chains and diverse revenue streams survived. Companies that had been dependent on a single revenue stream floundered.

- **The Shift in Capital Allocation**

Over the past decade, capital allocation in the GCC has shifted. Early on, capital flowed toward e-commerce and ride-hailing. Later, capital shifted toward fintech and healthtech. More recently, capital has shifted toward deeptech and enterprise software. Companies that adapted to these shifts thrived. Companies that didn't adapt struggled.

How to Navigate Sandstorms

Navigating sandstorms requires several capabilities:

1. Scenario Planning: Successful founders spend time thinking about what could go wrong. What if regulations change? What if capital flows shift? What if a competitor enters the market? What if a political shift changes the landscape? By thinking through scenarios, you're better prepared when sandstorms hit.

2. Flexible Business Models: Build business models that can adapt to changing conditions. Don't build a business that depends on a single revenue stream or a single market condition. Build flexibility into your model.

3. Strong Relationships: Your relationships with regulators, partners, customers, and investors are your shelter during sandstorms. When conditions change, these relationships help you navigate the change.

4. Financial Resilience: Build financial reserves. Don't spend every dollar you make. Instead, build cash reserves that allow you to weather downturns. Companies with strong financial reserves can adapt quickly when sandstorms hit, but cash-constrained companies struggle.

5. Speed of Adaptation: When sandstorms hit, the companies that adapt quickly survive. This means having decision-making processes that allow you to adapt quickly. It means having a culture that embraces change. It means having leaders who can make decisions under uncertainty.

The Sandstorm as Opportunity

Interestingly, sandstorms also create opportunities. When the landscape changes, old competitive advantages become less valuable while new competitive advantages emerge. Companies that understand the new landscape better than competitors can gain market share.

The founders who thrive during sandstorms are the ones who see them not just as threats, but as opportunities. They ask: 'How can we adapt to this new landscape better than our competitors? What new competitive advantages can we build?'

MENTAL MODEL 4: THE OASIS PRINCIPLE — SOLVE FRICTION, EARN LOYALTY

Every successful company solves a problem. But not all problem-solving leads to billion-dollar companies.

The difference is in the Oasis Principle.

What the Oasis Principle Teaches

In the desert, the oasis is the most valuable place. It's where people gather. It's where they refresh. It's where they prepare for the next leg of their journey. The oasis is valuable not just because it has water, but because it solves a critical problem: thirst, exhaustion, uncertainty.

In business, the Oasis Principle is similar. The most valuable companies are the ones that solve critical friction points in their customers' lives. They're the ones that become essential. They're the ones that customers return to again and again.

Identifying Your Oasis

What's the critical friction point you're solving? What's the problem that, when solved, makes your customer's life significantly better?

The most successful companies in the GCC are the ones that have identified a critical oasis:

- **Careem**: Solved the friction of getting reliable, safe transportation in the GCC. Became the oasis that customers returned to again and again.
- **Talabat**: Solved the friction of finding and ordering food from restaurants. Became the oasis that customers returned to again and again.
- **Tabby**: Solved the friction of managing cash flow and accessing credit. Became the oasis that customers returned to again and again.

Building Loyalty Through Your Oasis

When you solve a critical friction point, you earn loyalty. Not because of marketing. Not because of brand. But because you've made your customer's life better.

This loyalty is different from customer satisfaction. Customer satisfaction is transactional. Loyalty is emotional. It's the difference between a customer who uses your product because it's convenient and one who uses your product because they can't imagine using anything else.

The founders who build billion-dollar companies are the ones who understand that their job is to build an oasis—to solve a critical friction point so well that customers become loyal advocates.

The Oasis Principle in Practice
How do you apply the Oasis Principle?

1. Identify the Friction: What's the critical problem your customers face? What's the friction that makes their life difficult?

2. Solve it Completely: Don't partially solve the problem— solve it completely. Make it so good that customers can't imagine going back to the old way.

3. Make it Easy: The oasis isn't just water. It's water that's easy to access. So make your solution easy to use, easy to access, and easy to benefit from.

4. Become Essential: The goal is to become so essential that customers can't imagine their life without you. This is when you've *truly* built an oasis.

5. Expand From the Oasis: Once you've become essential in solving one friction point, you can expand to solve others. But don't expand until you've fully dominated your initial oasis.

MENTAL MODEL 5: THE GRAVITY EFFECT — FOUNDERS SHAPE ECOSYSTEMS

Here's something that separates founders who build billion-dollar companies from those who don't: they understand that they're not just building a company, but shaping an ecosystem.

This is the Gravity Effect.

What the Gravity Effect Teaches

In physics, gravity is a force that pulls objects toward a center. The stronger the center, the greater the pull.

In business, founders create gravity. Your vision, your energy, your discipline, your values—these things create a gravitational pull. They pull talent toward you. They pull customers toward you. They pull partners toward you. They pull investors toward you.

The strongest founders create the strongest gravity. They attract the best talent. They attract the best customers. They attract the best partners. They attract the best investors.

How Gravity Works

Gravity works through several mechanisms:

1. Vision: A clear, compelling vision creates gravity. People want to be part of something meaningful. When you have a clear vision of what you're building and why it matters, you create gravitational pull.

2. Execution: When you execute a plan well, you create gravity. You show that your vision is real. You show that you can deliver. You show that it's worth joining your company.

3. Culture: When you build a strong culture, you create gravity. People want to work in an environment where they feel valued, where they can do their best work, and where they're part of something meaningful.

4. Values: When you maintain your values consistently, you create gravity. People respect founders who stand for something. People want to work with founders who have integrity.

5. Momentum: When you build momentum, you create gravity. Success attracts success. When people see that you're winning, they want to be part of it.

The Gravity Effect in the GCC

In the GCC, the Gravity Effect is particularly powerful. Why? Because the region values strength and clarity. When you have a clear vision, execute well, and maintain your values, you create a gravitational pull that's difficult to resist.

The founders who build billion-dollar companies in the GCC are the ones who understand that they're shaping an ecosystem. They're not just building a company. They're creating a force that attracts the best talent, the best customers, the best partners, the best investors.

Building Your Gravity

How do you build gravity?

1. Develop a Clear Vision: Be clear about what you're building and why it matters. Make it compelling. Make it meaningful.

2. Execute Relentlessly: Show that your vision is real. Deliver results. Build momentum.

3. Build a Strong Culture: Create an environment where people want to work. Where they can do their best work. Where they're part of something meaningful.

4. Maintain Your Values: Stand for something. Have integrity. Be consistent.

5. Share Your Mission: Help others understand what you're building and why it matters. Create advocates. Create a movement.

When you do these things, you create gravity. You become a force. You attract the best people. You build a billion-dollar company.

Applying the Mental Models: From Theory to Practice

These five mental models—the Desert Model, the Trust Engine, the Sandstorm Principle, the Oasis Principle, and the Gravity Effect—are not abstract concepts. They're practical lenses that should guide your decisions every day.

WHEN YOU'RE DECIDING WHETHER TO ENTER A NEW MARKET:

Use the Desert Model. Ask yourself: Have I dominated my current market? Do I have the relationships I need in this new market? Am I prepared for the challenges of this new market? Or am I moving too fast?

WHEN YOU'RE DECIDING HOW TO TREAT A PARTNER OR CUSTOMER:

Use the Trust Engine. Ask yourself: Will this decision build or erode trust? Will this decision strengthen or weaken my reputation? Am I doing what I said I would do? Am I treating this person well?

WHEN MARKET CONDITIONS CHANGE SUDDENLY:

Use the Sandstorm Principle. Ask yourself: What's the new landscape? How do I adapt my business model? What new opportunities does this create? How do I move quickly while maintaining stability?

WHEN YOU'RE DECIDING WHAT PROBLEM TO SOLVE:

Use the Oasis Principle. Ask yourself: Is this a critical friction point? Will solving this make my customer's life significantly better? Can I become the oasis that customers return to again and again?

WHEN YOU'RE BUILDING YOUR TEAM AND YOUR CULTURE:

Use the Gravity Effect. Ask yourself: What vision am I creating? What culture am I building? What values am I maintaining? Am I creating gravitational pull that attracts the best people?

These mental models are your compass. They're not rules—they're lenses that help you see the landscape more clearly and make better decisions.

SUMMARY

Mental Models for Crossing the Desert

The Desert Model: Endurance Before Scale
- Move deliberately, not fast
- Survival comes before dominance
- Relationships are infrastructure
- Preparation matters
- Resilience is built into your DNA
- Once you dominate, stay dominant.

The Trust Engine: Reputation Compounds Faster Than Capital

- Your reputation precedes you
- Do what you say you're going to do
- Treat people well, even when inconvenient
- Be transparent about challenges
- Invest in relationships before you need them
- Maintain your values even when costly
- Your reputation is your most defensible competitive advantage.

The Sandstorm Principle: Adaptation Beats Speed

- Sandstorms are part of the landscape
- Scenario planning prepares you
- Build flexible business models
- Strong relationships are your shelter
- Financial resilience allows quick adaptation
- Speed of adaptation is critical
- Sandstorms create opportunities for those who adapt.

The Oasis Principle: Solve Friction, Earn Loyalty

- Identify the critical friction point
- Solve it completely
- Make it easy
- Become essential
- Expand from the oasis
- Loyalty comes from solving critical problems.

The Gravity Effect: Founders Shape Ecosystems
- Vision creates gravitational pull
- Execution creates gravitational pull
- Culture creates gravitational pull
- Values create gravitational pull
- Momentum creates gravitational pull
- You attract what you create.

These mental models are the thinking tools of billion-dollar founders. They're not theories. They're frameworks drawn from real experience. They're proven through real outcomes. They're how you think your way to billion-dollar scale.

CHAPTER 10

GLOBAL PRINCIPLES REWRITTEN FOR THE GCC

The Bridge Between Worlds

THE TEMPTATION TO COPY

One of the biggest mistakes I see GCC founders make is copying Silicon Valley wholesale.

They read about 'move fast and break things' and try to apply it directly. They read about 'fail fast' and try to apply it directly. They read about 'growth at all costs' and try to apply it directly.

But the GCC isn't Silicon Valley. The market is different. The culture is different. The regulatory environment is different. The customer expectations are different.

The most successful founders in the GCC are the ones who understand the best ideas from Silicon Valley and the rest of the world, but then adapt them for the GCC context. They take the principles and rewrite them for the region.

This is the bridge between worlds. This is how you build billion-dollar companies in the GCC.

PRINCIPLE 1: MOVE FAST → MOVE FAST WITHOUT BREAKING TRUST

The Silicon Valley Version

In Silicon Valley, the mantra is 'move fast and break things.' The idea is that speed is more important than perfection. It's better to move quickly and make mistakes than to move slowly and get everything right.

This makes sense in Silicon Valley for several reasons:
1. **The Market is Forgiving**: If you break something, you can usually fix it quickly. Customers are forgiving. Regulators are forgiving.
2. **Speed is a Competitive Advantage**: In a fast-moving market, the company that moves fastest often wins.
3. **Iteration is Valued**: The culture celebrates learning from mistakes and iterating quickly.

The GCC Version

In the GCC, the principle is: 'Move fast without breaking trust.'

Why? Because in the GCC, trust is your most valuable asset. When you break trust, you don't just lose a customer. You lose your reputation. You lose relationships. You lose opportunities.

This doesn't mean you move slowly. It means you move fast, but you're careful about what you break.

What This Means in Practice

- **Move Fast in Product Development**: Iterate rapidly. Test with customers. Learn quickly. This is where speed matters.
- **Move Fast in Market Expansion**: Enter new markets. Test new segments. Expand your reach. This is where speed matters.
- **Move Fast in Innovation**: Try new approaches. Experiment. Learn from what works and what doesn't. This is where speed matters.
- **Don't Move Fast with Trust**: Don't make promises you can't keep. Don't treat people poorly. Don't hide problems. Don't compromise your values. This is where you need to be careful.

The founders who succeed in the GCC are the ones who have learned to move fast in the right places and maintain stability in the places that matter most.

PRINCIPLE 2: FAIL FAST → LEARN FAST (BUT MAINTAIN REPUTATION)

The Silicon Valley Version
In Silicon Valley, the mantra is 'fail fast.' The idea is that failure is a learning opportunity. The faster you fail, the faster you learn. The culture celebrates failure as a necessary part of the journey.

This makes sense in Silicon Valley because:
1. **Capital is Abundant**: If you fail, you can raise more capital and try again.
2. **Failure is Normalized**: Everyone fails. It's part of the journey. There's no shame in it.

3. **Pivoting is Celebrated**: If your original idea doesn't work, you pivot. The culture celebrates founders who can adapt.

The GCC Version
In the GCC, the principle is: 'Learn fast, but maintain your reputation.'

Why? Because in the GCC, your reputation follows you. If you fail publicly and blame others, if you fail without learning, if you fail and move on without taking responsibility—your reputation suffers.

This doesn't mean you don't fail. It means you fail thoughtfully. You learn from your failures. You take responsibility. You maintain your reputation, even in failure.

What This Means in Practice

- **Fail in Private, Learn in Public**: Don't broadcast every failure. But when you learn something important, share it. Help others learn from your mistakes.
- **Take Responsibility**: When something fails, take responsibility. Don't blame others. Don't make excuses. Take responsibility and learn.
- **Learn Deeply**: Don't just move on from failure. Understand why it failed. Extract the lessons. Apply those lessons to your next venture.
- **Maintain Relationships**: Even in failure, maintain your relationships. Treat people well. Communicate honestly. Maintain trust.
- **Pivot Thoughtfully**: If your original idea doesn't work, pivot. But don't pivot randomly. Pivot based on what you've learned. Pivot with a clear understanding of why you're changing direction.

The founders who succeed in the GCC are the ones who have learned to fail fast but maintain their reputation. They learn quickly, but they do it in a way that preserves trust and relationships.

PRINCIPLE 3: GROWTH AT ALL COSTS → SMART GROWTH IN REGULATED MARKETS

The Silicon Valley Version

In Silicon Valley, the mantra is 'growth at all costs.' The idea is that growth is the most important metric. Everything else is secondary. Get big fast. Worry about profitability later. Worry about regulation later.

This makes sense in Silicon Valley because:

1. **The Market is Large and Relatively Unregulated**: You can grow rapidly without hitting regulatory constraints.
2. **Capital is Abundant**: If you're growing fast, capital will follow.
3. **First-mover Advantage is Valuable**: The company that grows fastest often wins.

The GCC Version

In the GCC, the principle is: 'Smart growth in regulated markets.'

Why? Because the GCC market is smaller, more regulated, and more relationship-dependent. Growing too fast can trigger regulatory scrutiny. Growing too fast can damage relationships. Growing too fast can create operational challenges that undermine your foundation.

This doesn't mean you grow slowly. It means you grow intelligently. You grow in a way that's sustainable. You grow in a way that maintains your competitive advantages. You grow in a way that doesn't trigger regulatory problems.

What This Means in Practice

- **Understand the Regulatory Environment**: Before you grow, understand the regulatory landscape. Know what's allowed and what's not. Build compliance into your growth strategy.
- **Build Relationships with Regulators**: Don't wait until you have a problem to build relationships with regulators. Build relationships proactively. Help regulators understand what you're doing. Get their input.
- **Grow Sustainably**: Don't grow so fast that you can't maintain quality. Don't grow so fast that you can't maintain your culture. Don't grow so fast that you burn through capital unsustainably.
- **Focus on Unit Economics**: Make sure that every unit of growth is profitable. Don't sacrifice unit economics for growth. Build a business that can scale profitably.
- **Maintain Your Competitive Advantages**: As you grow, maintain the competitive advantages that made you successful. Don't sacrifice what makes you special for the sake of growth.

The founders who succeed in the GCC are the ones who have learned to grow fast, but smartly. They grow in a way that's sustainable, compliant, and profitable.

PRINCIPLE 4: CULTURE AS PERK → CULTURE AS OPERATING SYSTEM

The Silicon Valley Version

In Silicon Valley, culture is often treated as a perk. Free food. Free drinks. Ping pong tables. Flexible hours. The idea is that if you make work fun, people will want to work for you.

This makes sense in Silicon Valley because:

1. **Competition for Talent is Intense**: You need perks to attract talent.
2. **Talent is Mobile**: If people don't like your culture, they can leave and find another job easily.
3. **Perks are Visible**: They're easy to implement and easy to see.

The GCC Version

In the GCC, the principle is: 'Culture as operating system.'

Why? Because in the GCC, culture isn't just about making work fun. It's about how you make decisions. It's about how you treat people. It's about how you maintain your values as you scale. It's about how you build a company that lasts.

This doesn't mean you don't have perks. It means that culture is much deeper than perks. Culture is the foundation of how your company operates.

What This Means in Practice

- **Define Your Values Clearly**: Be clear about what your company stands for. What are your core values? How do these values guide your decisions?
- **Hire for Culture Fit**: Don't just hire for skills. Hire for culture fit. Hire people who share your values. Hire people who will maintain your culture as you scale.
- **Make Decisions Based on Your Values**: When you face difficult decisions, let your values guide you. This consistency builds a strong culture.
- **Invest in Your People**: In the GCC, where talent is scarce, investing in your people is critical. Invest in their development. Invest in their growth. Invest in their wellbeing.
- **Maintain Your Culture as You Scale**: As you grow, your culture will be tested. New people will join. New challenges will emerge. Maintain your culture intentionally. Don't let it dilute as you scale.
- **Make Culture Visible**: Don't just talk about your culture. Make it visible through your decisions, your actions, your investments. Let people see your culture in action.

The founders who succeed in the GCC are the ones who have built culture as an operating system. They've built a culture that guides their decisions, that attracts talent, that maintains their values as they scale.

PRINCIPLE 5: PRODUCT-FIRST → RELATIONSHIP-FIRST AND PRODUCT-FIRST

The Silicon Valley Version

In Silicon Valley, the mantra is 'product first.' The idea is that if you build a great product, everything else will follow. Focus on the product. Make it great. The rest will take care of itself.

This makes sense in Silicon Valley because:

1. **The Market is Large and Impersonal**: You can succeed with a great product even if you don't have relationships.
2. **Distribution is Digital**: You can reach customers digitally without relationships.
3. **The Culture Values Innovation**: The culture celebrates founders who focus on building great products.

The GCC Version

In the GCC, the principle is: 'Relationship first *and* product first.'

Why? Because in the GCC, relationships are infrastructure. You can't succeed with a great product if you don't have relationships with regulators, with partners, with customers, with investors.

This doesn't mean your product doesn't matter. It means that relationships are equally important. You need both.

What This Means in Practice

- **Build Relationships with Regulators**: Before you build your product, build relationships with regulators. Understand the regulatory environment. Get their input. Help them understand what you're building.

- **Build Relationships with Customers**: Don't just build a product and hope customers will come. Build relationships with customers. Understand their needs. Get their input. Make them part of your journey.

- **Build Relationships with Partners**: Identify potential partners early. Build relationships with them. Help them understand what you're building. Explore how you can work together.

- **Build Relationships with Investors**: Don't just pitch investors when you need capital. Build relationships with investors early. Help them understand your vision. Get their input.

- **Build a Great Product**: While you're building relationships, build a great product. Make it solve a real problem. Make it better than alternatives. Make it something customers love.

- **Let Relationships and Product Reinforce Each Other**: The best companies are the ones where relationships and product reinforce each other. Your relationships help you build a better product. Your product helps you build stronger relationships.

The founders who succeed in the GCC are the ones who have understood that success requires both relationships and a great product. They've built both simultaneously.

PRINCIPLE 6: DISRUPTION AT ANY COST → CONTRIBUTION AND EXCELLENCE

The Silicon Valley Version

In Silicon Valley, the mantra is 'disruption.' The idea is that the best companies are the ones that disrupt existing markets. The culture celebrates founders who challenge the status quo, who break the rules, who do things that have never been done before.

This makes sense in Silicon Valley because:
1. **Disruption is Rewarded**: The most successful companies are often the ones that disrupted existing markets.
2. **The Culture Celebrates Rebels**: The culture celebrates founders who challenge the status quo.
3. **Disruption Creates Competitive Advantages**: When you disrupt, you create advantages that competitors can't easily replicate.

The GCC Version

In the GCC, the principle is: 'Contribution and excellence.'

Why? Because in the GCC, the most successful companies are the ones that contribute to the region's transformation while maintaining excellence in execution. The culture values founders who are solving real problems, who are contributing to economic diversification, who are maintaining high standards.

This doesn't mean you don't disrupt. It means that disruption is in service of contribution and excellence, not disruption for its own sake.

What This Means in Practice

- **Identify the Problem You're Solving**: Be clear about what problem you're solving. How does solving this problem contribute to the region's transformation?
- **Maintain High Standards**: Don't disrupt just for the sake of disruption. Disrupt in a way that maintains high standards. Build something excellent.
- **Contribute to the Region**: Think about how your company is contributing to the region's transformation. Are you creating jobs? Are you developing talent? Are you solving problems that matter to the region?
- **Build for the Long Term**: Don't disrupt in a way that creates short-term chaos. Disrupt in a way that builds something lasting. Build for the long term.
- Maintain Relationships: Don't disrupt in a way that damages relationships. Disrupt in a way that maintains trust. Disrupt in a way that brings people along with you.

The founders who succeed in the GCC are the ones who have understood that the best disruption is disruption in service of contribution and excellence. They're not disrupting for its own sake. They're disrupting to solve real problems and contribute to the region's transformation.

THE BRIDGE BETWEEN WORLDS

Here's what I want you to understand: the GCC is not Silicon Valley. But it's not a rejection of Silicon Valley principles either. It's an adaptation.

The most successful founders in the GCC are the ones who have taken the best principles from Silicon Valley and the rest of the world, but who have adapted them for the GCC context.

They've learned to:
- Move fast without breaking trust
- Learn fast while maintaining reputation
- Grow smartly in regulated markets
- Build culture as an operating system
- Combine relationships and product
- Disrupt in service of contribution and excellence.

These founders are building the bridge between worlds. They're taking global principles and making them local. They're taking local wisdom and making it global.

This is how you build billion-dollar companies in the GCC. This is how you become a founder who can compete globally while thriving locally.

SUMMARY

Global Principles Rewritten for the GCC

Move Fast → Move Fast Without Breaking Trust

- Speed matters in product development, market expansion, innovation
- Stability matters in trust, relationships, values
- Don't sacrifice trust for speed

Fail Fast → Learn Fast (But Maintain Reputation)

- Fail in private, learn in public
- Take responsibility for failures
- Learn deeply from mistakes
- Maintain relationships even in failure
- Pivot thoughtfully based on learning

Growth at All Costs → Smart Growth in Regulated Markets

- Understand the regulatory environment
- Build relationships with regulators
- Grow sustainably
- Focus on unit economics
- Maintain your competitive advantages

Culture as Perk → Culture as Operating System

- Define your values clearly
- Hire for culture fit
- Make decisions based on your values
- Invest in your people
- Maintain your culture as you scale

Product First → Relationship First and Product First
- Build relationships with regulators, customers, partners, investors
- Build a great product
- Let relationships and product reinforce each other
- Success requires both

Disruption at Any Cost → Contribution and Excellence
- Identify the problem you're solving
- Maintain high standards
- Contribute to the region
- Build for the long term
- Maintain relationships.

These are the principles that bridge Silicon Valley and the GCC. These are the principles that allow you to compete globally while thriving locally. These are the principles that build billion-dollar companies in the GCC.

PART 4

The GCC Blueprint for Building Enduring Companies

This part of the playbook equips founders with critical knowledge for scaling their businesses through effective growth strategies, marketing approaches, and funding options. By understanding the landscape of investors, mastering the art of pitching, and developing a solid roadmap for scale, entrepreneurs can position themselves for success in their journey toward becoming billion-dollar enterprises. Each chapter provides practical guidance to navigate the complexities of funding and strategic growth, reinforcing the importance of a well-defined plan to achieve lasting impact.

CHAPTER 11

THE GCC OPPORTUNITY MAP

Why This Is Your Moment

THE FOUNDER'S ERA IS BEGINNING

We are entering a new era in the GCC. An era where founders—not just family businesses, not just government initiatives, not just foreign companies—are building the region's future.

This is the Founder's Era.

For decades, the GCC economy was shaped by oil and gas. Then it was shaped by government initiatives and sovereign wealth funds. Then it was shaped by foreign companies entering the region.

But now, something is shifting. Founders are emerging. They're building companies that are solving real problems. They're building companies that are contributing to economic diversification. They're building companies that are competing globally while thriving locally.

This shift is not accidental. It's the result of converging forces. Capital is available. Technology is accessible. Government is supportive. Customers are ready. The time is now.

This chapter is about understanding the landscape. It's about seeing the opportunity. It's about understanding why the GCC is the next frontier for billion-dollar companies.

THE NUMBERS: WHY THE GCC IS UNIQUE

$3.5 Trillion in Sovereign Wealth Funds

The GCC countries collectively manage over $3.5 trillion in sovereign wealth funds. This is capital that's actively looking for investment opportunities. This is capital that's committed to economic diversification. This is capital that's available to founders who can demonstrate vision and execution.

To put this in perspective: This is more capital than the total venture capital deployed globally in the past five years. This is capital that's looking for the next generation of billion-dollar companies.

A Young, Digital-Native Population

The GCC has one of the youngest populations in the world. Over 60% of the population is under 35 years old. This is a population that grew up with smartphones. This is a population that's comfortable with digital-first products and services. This is a population that's hungry for innovation.

More importantly, this is a population with disposable income. Unlike many emerging markets, the GCC population has purchasing power. They're willing to spend on products and services they value.

Massive Digital Adoption

The GCC has some of the highest digital adoption rates in the world. Over 90% of the population in the UAE and Qatar has internet access. Smartphone penetration is above 80% in most GCC countries. Social media usage is among the highest globally.

This digital infrastructure creates opportunities for digital-first businesses. It creates opportunities for e-commerce, for fintech, for healthtech, for edtech, for any business that can serve customers digitally.

National Digital Transformation Mandates

Every GCC government has committed to digital transformation. Saudi Arabia has Vision 2030. The UAE has Centennial 2071. Qatar has National Vision 2030. Kuwait, Bahrain, and Oman all have similar initiatives.

These aren't just aspirational statements. They're backed by substantial government resources. They're driving policy changes. They're creating regulatory sandboxes. They're funding innovation initiatives. They're creating an environment where innovation is not just welcomed—it's mandated.

Underserved Categories

Many sectors in the GCC are still underserved. E-commerce penetration is lower than in developed markets. Fintech adoption is still early. Healthtech is emerging. Edtech is growing. Enterprise software is underdeveloped. There are opportunities in almost every sector.

Rise of Regional Tech Champions

The GCC has already produced several tech champions: Careem, Talabat, Tabby, Souq.com, and others. These companies have proven that billion-dollar companies can be built in the region. They've shown that founders can compete globally while thriving locally. They've created a template for success.

The Shift from Consumers to Creators, from Operators to Builders

For years, the GCC was primarily a market for consumption. People consumed products built elsewhere. But now, the region is shifting. People are becoming creators. They're becoming builders. They're starting companies. They're building products. They're contributing to the region's transformation.

This shift is profound. It's changing the culture. It's changing the incentives. It's creating opportunities for founders who can tap into this shift.

THE OPPORTUNITY MAP: WHERE TO BUILD

Within this broader opportunity, certain sectors are poised for particularly explosive growth:

Fintech and Financial Services

The GCC is undergoing a fintech revolution. Digital payments are growing rapidly. Buy now, pay later is becoming mainstream. Digital banking is expanding. Blockchain and cryptocurrency are being explored. Islamic fintech is emerging.

Companies like Tabby and Tamara have already achieved unicorn status. But the market is still in its early stages. There are opportunities for founders to build the next generation of fintech companies.

Healthtech and Digital Health

The GCC governments are prioritizing healthcare quality and accessibility. Telemedicine is expanding. Digital health records are being implemented. AI-powered diagnostics are emerging. Wellness and preventative health are becoming priorities.

The COVID-19 pandemic accelerated digital health adoption. But the market is still developing. There are opportunities for founders to build the next generation of healthtech companies.

Edtech and Digital Learning

The GCC has a young population that's hungry for education and skill development. The region's economic diversification requires a workforce with new skills. Edtech companies are emerging. Digital learning platforms are growing. Vocational training is expanding.

The market is still developing. There are opportunities for founders to build the next generation of edtech companies.

E-commerce and Logistics

E-commerce is growing rapidly in the GCC, but the market is still fragmented. There are opportunities for founders to build better e-commerce platforms, better logistics solutions, better supply chain technologies.

Companies like Noon and Souq.com have already achieved significant scale, but the market is still expanding. There are opportunities for founders to build the next generation of e-commerce companies.

Deeptech and Enterprise Software

The GCC is investing heavily in AI, robotics, blockchain, and other deep technologies, but the region still has a gap in deeptech and enterprise software. There are opportunities for founders to build deeptech companies that serve the region's needs.

Tourism and Hospitality Tech

The GCC is positioning itself as a global tourism destination. Saudi Arabia is opening to tourism. The UAE is expanding tourism. Qatar is investing in tourism infrastructure. There are opportunities for founders to build tourism and hospitality tech companies.

Climate Tech and Sustainability

The GCC is facing unique climate challenges. Water scarcity, energy efficiency, waste management, and sustainable development are becoming priorities. There are opportunities for founders to build climate tech companies that address these challenges.

Creator Economy and Content

The GCC has a vibrant creator economy. Content creators, influencers, and digital creators are emerging. There are opportunities for founders to build platforms and tools that serve the creator economy.

The Competitive Advantages of Building in the GCC Now

If you're a founder in the GCC right now, you have advantages that founders in other regions don't have:

First-Mover Advantage

In many sectors, there's still time to be a first-mover or early mover. The founders who move quickly and execute well can establish market leadership that's difficult to challenge. This window won't stay open forever. But right now, it's open.

Relationship Advantages

In a relationship-driven business culture, your ability to build relationships is your competitive advantage. Global founders struggle with this. They don't have the cultural understanding. They don't have the networks. They don't have the relationships. *You* have these advantages.

Market Understanding

You understand the GCC market in ways that global competitors don't. You understand the regulatory landscape. You understand the cultural nuances. You understand the customer preferences. You understand the business practices. This market understanding is a defensible competitive advantage.

Capital Access

Capital is available to founders with vision and execution. You have access to angel investors, venture capitalists, strategic investors, and sovereign wealth funds. You have access to capital that global founders in other regions don't have.

Government Support

GCC governments are actively supporting innovation. There are accelerator programs, regulatory sandboxes, tax incentives, and other support mechanisms. You have access to government support that founders in other regions don't have.

Talent Access
The GCC attracts talent from around the world. You have access to talented people from diverse backgrounds. You can build teams that combine local knowledge with global expertise.

The Window is Open
The combination of these advantages creates a unique window of opportunity. This window won't stay open forever. As the market matures, as competition increases, as first-mover advantages are captured, the window will close.

But right now, the window is open. The question is: will you step through it?

THE FOUNDER'S ADVANTAGE: WHY YOU CAN WIN
Here's what I want you to understand: You have advantages that global founders don't have. But you also have challenges that global founders don't face.

The global founders have scale. They have brand recognition. They have capital. They have experience.

But you have something they don't: you understand the market. You understand the culture. You understand the relationships. You understand what it takes to succeed in the GCC.

This is your advantage. This is why you can win.

The Founders Who Will Win

The founders who will win in the GCC are the ones who:

1. **Understand the market deeply**: They understand the regulatory landscape. They understand the cultural nuances. They understand the customer preferences.
2. **Build relationships intentionally**: They build relationships with regulators, with partners, with customers, with investors. They understand that relationships are infrastructure.
3. **Execute with discipline**: They have systems. They have processes. They have the ability to execute consistently.
4. **Maintain their values**: They're clear about what they stand for. They maintain their values even when it's costly.
5. **Think long-term**: They're building companies that will last for decades, not companies designed for a quick exit.
6. **Contribute to the region**: They're solving problems that matter to the region. They're contributing to economic diversification.

If you have these characteristics, you can win. You can build a billion-dollar company in the GCC.

The Moment We're In

We are in a unique moment in the GCC's history. A moment where:

- Capital is abundant
- Government is supportive
- Customers are ready

- Technology is accessible
- Talent is available
- Opportunities are everywhere.

This moment won't last forever. The market will mature. Competition will increase. First-mover advantages will be captured. The window will close.

But right now, the window is open. Right now is your moment.

The question is: what will you do with it?

SUMMARY

The GCC Opportunity Map
- The Founder's Era Is Beginning
- Founders are emerging as builders of the region's future
- This shift is the result of converging forces
- Capital, technology, government support, and customer readiness are all aligned

The Numbers
- $3.5 trillion in sovereign wealth funds
- Young, digital-native population
- Massive digital adoption
- National digital transformation mandates
- Underserved categories
- Rise of regional tech champions
- Shift from consumers to creators

The Opportunity Map

- Fintech and financial services
- Healthtech and digital health
- Edtech and digital learning
- E-commerce and logistics
- Deeptech and enterprise software
- Tourism and hospitality tech
- Climate tech and sustainability
- Creator economy and content

Your Competitive Advantages

- First-mover advantage
- Relationship advantages
- Market understanding
- Capital access
- Government support
- Talent access

Why You Can Win

- You understand the market deeply
- You build relationships intentionally
- You execute with discipline
- You maintain your values
- You think long-term
- You contribute to the region

The Moment We're In

- Capital is abundant
- Government is supportive
- Customers are ready
- Technology is accessible
- Talent is available
- Opportunities are everywhere.

This is your moment. The window is open. The time to build is now.

CHAPTER 12

THE RISE OF THE UNI-CAMEL

The Movement Begins

WHY THE CAMEL, NOT THE UNICORN?

Unicorns Are Fragile

Unicorns are mythical creatures. They don't exist in nature. They're not built for harsh conditions. They're not built to survive challenges.

Many unicorns in the startup world are fragile in the same way. They're built for a specific market condition. They're dependent on continuous capital infusions. They're dependent on rapid growth. They're dependent on a specific regulatory environment. When conditions change, they struggle.

Camels Are Resilient

Camels are built for harsh conditions. They survive in the desert. They endure droughts. They cross vast distances. They carry heavy loads. They're built to last.

The companies that will thrive in the GCC are the ones that are built like camels. They're resilient. They can survive market downturns. They can adapt to regulatory changes. They can endure challenges. They can carry the region forward.

Unicorns Are Temporary

Most unicorns are temporary. They're built to be acquired or to go public. They're built for an exit. They're built for a specific time horizon—typically 5–10 years.

Camels Are Enduring

Camels live for decades. They carry generations. They're built to endure.

The companies that will define the GCC are the ones that are built to endure. They're built to last for decades. They're built to evolve and adapt. They're built to serve generations of customers.

Unicorns Are Imported

The unicorn metaphor is imported from Silicon Valley. It reflects Silicon Valley values—rapid growth, disruption, exits. But these values don't reflect GCC values.

Camels Are Native

The camel is native to the GCC. It reflects the region's values—resilience, endurance, adaptation, survival. It reflects the region's history. It reflects the region's identity.

When we talk about building Uni-Camels, we're not just talking about building billion-dollar companies. We're talking about building companies that are rooted in the region. Companies that reflect the region's values. Companies that carry the region's identity into the future.

What Is a Uni-Camel?

A Uni-Camel is a billion-dollar company that's built like a camel. It has specific characteristics:

Resilient

A Uni-Camel is built to survive challenges. It's not dependent on a single revenue stream. It's not dependent on a single market condition. It's built with flexibility. It's built with financial reserves. It's built to weather downturns, regulatory changes, competitive challenges, and unexpected crises.

Enduring

A Uni-Camel is built to last for decades. It's not built for a quick exit. It's built to evolve and adapt. It's built to serve generations of customers. It's built to be a lasting institution in the region.

Adapted to the GCC

A Uni-Camel is built with deep understanding of the GCC market. It reflects the region's values. It serves the region's needs. It contributes to the region's transformation. It's not a global company operating in the GCC. It's a GCC company that understands the region deeply.

Carrying the Region Forward

A Uni-Camel is built to contribute to the region's transformation. It creates high-quality jobs. It develops local talent. It solves problems that matter to the region. It contributes to economic diversification. It carries the region forward.

Globally Competitive

A Uni-Camel is built to compete globally. It has world-class products and services. It has international standards of excellence. It represents the region on the global stage. It shows the world what the GCC is capable of.

Locally Rooted

A Uni-Camel is built with deep roots in the region. It's built on relationships. It's built on cultural understanding. It's built on local talent and local expertise. It's not a foreign company. It's a GCC company.

EXAMPLES OF UNI-CAMELS

Careem

Careem is a Uni-Camel. It's resilient—it survived regulatory challenges, competitive pressure, and market downturns. It's enduring—it's been operating for over a decade and continues to evolve. It's adapted to the GCC—it understood local preferences and built a product that resonated culturally. It's carried the region forward—it created thousands of jobs and developed local talent. It's globally competitive—it competed with Uber and won in the region. It's locally rooted—it was built by founders who understood the region deeply.

Talabat

Talabat is a Uni-Camel. It's resilient—it survived market challenges and competitive pressure. It's enduring—it's been operating for over a decade and continues to grow. It's adapted to the GCC—it understood how people eat and order food in the region. It's carried the region forward— it created jobs and developed the food delivery ecosystem. It's globally competitive—it competes with global players. It's locally rooted—it was built by founders who understood the region.

Tabby

Tabby is a Uni-Camel. It's resilient—it navigated the fintech landscape and regulatory challenges. It's enduring—it's built for the long term. It's adapted to the GCC—it understood how people manage cash flow and access credit in the region. It's carried the region forward—it's enabling financial inclusion. It's globally competitive—it competes with global fintech players. It's locally rooted—it was built by founders who understood the region.

Aramco

Aramco is a Uni-Camel. It's resilient—it survived oil price collapses and market challenges. It's enduring—it's been operating for over 80 years. It's adapted to the GCC— it's deeply rooted in Saudi Arabia. It's carried the region forward—it's been central to the region's development. It's globally competitive—it competes on the global stage. It's locally rooted—it's a Saudi company.

These companies show what's possible. They show that Uni-Camels can be built in the GCC. They show that founders can build billion-dollar companies that are resilient, enduring, adapted to the region, and globally competitive.

THE MOVEMENT: ANYONE CAN BUILD A UNI-CAMEL

Here's the most important insight: *Anyone* in the GCC can build a Uni-Camel.

It's not just for people with MBAs from top universities. It's not just for people with connections to wealthy families. It's not just for people with prior startup experience.

It's for:

Founders

People with an idea and the ambition to build a billion-dollar company. People who see a problem and want to solve it at scale. People who want to contribute to the region's transformation.

Students

Young people who see an opportunity and have the courage to pursue it. People who are just starting their careers but have big ambitions. People who want to build something meaningful.

Employees

People working in existing companies who see a better way and have the courage to start something new. People who have learned from others and want to apply those lessons. People who want to build something of their own.

Family Business Successors

People inheriting family businesses who want to transform them for the digital age. People who want to take what their families built and evolve it. People who want to build on a foundation of trust and relationships.

Creators

Artists, designers, engineers, and other creative people who want to build companies around their craft. People who have unique talents and want to scale them. People who want to build businesses around their passion.

Professionals

Doctors, lawyers, consultants, and other professionals who want to build companies around their expertise. People who have deep domain knowledge and want to apply it. People who want to solve problems in their industry.

The GCC needs Uni-Camels from all these groups. The region needs diverse founders building diverse companies which are solving diverse problems.

The movement is about democratizing billion-dollar ambition. It's about showing that anyone in the GCC can build a Uni-Camel if they have the vision, the discipline, and the courage to pursue it.

THE VALUES THAT WILL DEFINE UNI-CAMELS

As we look to the future, certain values will define the Uni-Camels that succeed:

Resilience Over Rapid Growth

Companies that prioritize sustainable, resilient growth will outperform companies that prioritize rapid growth at any cost. Companies that can survive downturns will thrive in the long term.

Trust Over Disruption

Companies that build trust with customers, partners, and regulators will outperform companies that try to disrupt at any cost. In the GCC, trust is your most valuable asset.

Purpose Over Profit

Companies that are clear about their purpose—what problem they're solving, what value they're creating—will outperform companies that are focused solely on profit. Purpose attracts talent. Purpose attracts customers. Purpose attracts investors.

Local Understanding Over Global Templates

Companies that understand the GCC market deeply and adapt their approach accordingly will outperform companies that try to apply global templates without adaptation. Local understanding is a defensible competitive advantage.

Endurance Over Exit

Companies that are built to endure and evolve will outperform companies that are built for a quick exit. Enduring companies create more value. They create more jobs. They contribute more to the region.

Contribution Over Extraction

Companies that are focused on contributing to the region's transformation will outperform companies that are focused on extracting value from the region. Contribution builds relationships. Contribution builds trust. Contribution builds a movement.

YOUR ROLE IN THE MOVEMENT

You're not just building a company. You're part of a movement. You're part of the transformation of the GCC.

Your role in this movement is to:

Build a Uni-Camel
Build a company that's resilient, enduring, adapted to the GCC, globally competitive, and locally rooted. Build a company that will carry the region forward.

Show What's Possible
By building a successful Uni-Camel, you show others what's possible. You inspire the next generation of founders. You demonstrate that billion-dollar companies can be built in the GCC.

Contribute to the Region's Transformation
By solving problems that matter to the region, by creating high-quality jobs, by developing local talent, by contributing to economic diversification, you help the region achieve its vision.

Mentor the Next Generation
By sharing your lessons, your insights, your experiences, you help the next generation of founders avoid your mistakes and accelerate their success.

Build a Community
By connecting with other founders, by sharing knowledge, by supporting each other, you build a community of Uni-Camel builders. This community is stronger than any individual company.

THE CALL: BUILD YOUR UNI-CAMEL

This is my call to you: Build your Uni-Camel.

Not because it's easy. Not because it's guaranteed to succeed. But because:

1. **The moment is now**: Capital is abundant. Government is supportive. Customers are ready. The window is open.
2. **You have advantages**: You understand the market. You have relationships. You have access to capital. You have government support.
3. **The region needs you**: The GCC needs founders who understand the market deeply. The region needs companies that are resilient and enduring. The region needs companies that contribute to its transformation.
4. **You can inspire others**: By building a successful Uni-Camel, you inspire the next generation. You show what's possible. You build a movement.
5. **It's meaningful**: Building a company that contributes to the region's transformation is meaningful. It's not just about making money. It's about building something that lasts. It's about contributing to something larger than yourself.

THE BEGINNING

This is not the end of your journey. This is the beginning.

You've read this book. You've learned the principles. You've seen the examples. You've understood the roadmap. You've understood the opportunity.

Now it's time to act.

Here's what I want you to do:

First: Take time to develop your strategic worldview. Understand your lens. Understand your constraints. Understand your long-term vision. Understand how you'll build relationships. Understand how you'll adapt culturally. Understand your philosophical principles.

Second: Define your idea. What problem are you solving? Who are you solving it for? Why does it matter? Be clear about your purpose.

Third: Talk to your first customers. Don't build in isolation. Get out and talk to real people who have the problem you're trying to solve.

Fourth: Build your MVP. Don't wait for perfection. Build something simple that solves the core problem.

Fifth: Validate your assumptions. Before committing significant capital, validate that your core assumptions are correct.

Sixth: Raise your first capital. Once you've achieved initial traction, raise capital strategically.

Seventh: Scale your vision. Execute with discipline. Dominate your initial market. Expand regionally. Build competitive advantages.

Eighth: Build your team. Surround yourself with exceptional people who share your vision.

Ninth: Maintain your vision. As you scale, stay focused on your core mission.

Tenth: Mentor the next generation. Share your lessons. Help others build their Uni-Camels.

FINAL THOUGHT: THE DREAM IS YOURS — WILL YOU BUILD IT?

The Uni-Camel is not just a metaphor. It's a movement. It's a declaration that the GCC is ready to produce billion-dollar companies. It's a declaration that founders in the region can compete globally while thriving locally. It's a declaration that the future of the GCC is being built by founders who understand the region deeply.

You are part of this movement. You are part of building the future of the GCC.

The question is: What will you build?

Go build your Uni-Camel.

CONCLUSION

THE VISION: THE GCC IN 2035

Imagine the GCC in 2035.

Imagine a region where there are dozens of billion-dollar companies. Companies that were built by founders who understood the region deeply. Companies that are resilient and enduring. Companies that are contributing to the region's transformation.

Imagine a region where entrepreneurship is celebrated. Where founders are mentors to the next generation. Where the startup ecosystem is thriving. Where capital is flowing to innovative companies. Where talent is developing. Where the region is known globally for its innovation and entrepreneurship.

Imagine a region where economic diversification is a reality. Where the economy is no longer dependent on oil and gas.

Where technology, tourism, finance, and other sectors are thriving. Where high-quality jobs are being created. Where local talent is being developed.

Imagine a region where Uni-Camels are walking across the desert, carrying the region forward.

This is the future we're building together. This is the movement we're part of.

THE RISE OF THE UNI-CAMEL

A Symbol for Our Time
- The camel is a symbol of the GCC: resilience, endurance, adaptation, survival
- The Uni-Camel is a billion-dollar company built like a camel
- Not a unicorn (fragile, temporary, imported), but a camel (resilient, enduring, native).

What Is a Uni-Camel?
- **Resilient**: survives challenges and downturns
- **Enduring**: built to last for decades
- **Adapted to the GCC**: reflects regional values and needs
- **Carrying the region forward**: contributes to transformation
- **Globally competitive**: world-class products and standards
- **Locally rooted**: deep relationships and understanding.

Examples of Uni-Camels

- **Careem**: resilient, enduring, adapted, contributing, competitive, rooted
- **Talabat**: resilient, enduring, adapted, contributing, competitive, rooted
- **Tabby**: resilient, enduring, adapted, contributing, competitive, rooted
- **Aramco**: resilient, enduring, adapted, contributing, competitive, rooted.

The Movement: Anyone Can Build a Uni-Camel

- Founders, students, employees, family business successors, creators, professionals
- Democratizing billion-dollar ambition
- The region needs diverse founders building diverse companies.

The Values That Will Define Uni-Camels

- Resilience over rapid growth
- Trust over disruption
- Purpose over profit
- Local understanding over global templates
- Endurance over exit
- Contribution over extraction.

Your Role in the Movement

- Build a Uni-Camel
- Show what's possible
- Contribute to the region's transformation
- Mentor the next generation
- Build a community.

The Vision: The GCC in 2035

- Dozens of billion-dollar companies
- Entrepreneurship celebrated
- Startup ecosystem thriving
- Economic diversification a reality
- Uni-Camels walking across the desert.

The Call to Action

- Build your Uni-Camel
- The moment is now
- You have advantages
- The region needs you
- You can inspire others
- It's meaningful.

This is the beginning of your journey.
Go build your Uni-Camel.

REFERENCES

CAREEM ACQUISITION BY UBER

CLAIM: 'Careem, the ride-hailing service that was acquired by Uber for a staggering $3.1 billion'

VERIFIED DETAILS:
- **Acquisition Amount**: $3.1 billion (confirmed)
- **Structure**: 1.7billionincash+1.4 billion in convertible notes
- **Announcement Date**: March 26, 2019
- **Completion Date**: January 2, 2020
- **Sources**:
  - Uber official press release (investor.uber.com)
  - Reuters, Forbes, Bloomberg reports
  - SEC filings.

SOUQ.COM ACQUISITION BY AMAZON

CLAIM: 'Souq.com, an e-commerce giant, was acquired by Amazon'

VERIFIED DETAILS:
- **Acquisition Confirmed**: Yes, Amazon acquired Souq.com
- **Acquisition Amount**: $580 million (final amount)
- **Announcement Date**: March 28, 2017
- **Completion Date**: July 3, 2017
- **Note**: Initial reports varied between 580M−650M, but official completion was at $580M
- **Sources**:
  - Amazon official announcements
  - TechCrunch, GeekWire, CNBC reports
  - Wikipedia entry

- **RECOMMENDATION**: Consider adding the acquisition amount ($580 million) for completeness and credibility.

KITOPI UNICORN STATUS

CLAIM: 'Kitopi, a leading cloud kitchen platform, which achieved unicorn status'

VERIFIED DETAILS:
- **Unicorn Status**: Confirmed (valuation >$1 billion)

- **Initial Unicorn Valuation**: $1 billion (July 2021)
- **Current Valuation**: $1.55 billion (May 2022)
- **Funding Rounds**:
  - Series C: $415 million (July 2021) - achieved unicorn status
  - Series C Extension: $300 million (May 2022)
  - Lead Investor: SoftBank Vision Fund 2

- **Sources**:
  - Bloomberg, TechCrunch reports
  - Company announcements
  - Multiple venture capital databases.

TABBY AND TAMARA BNPL MARKET POSITION

CLAIM: 'Companies like Tabby and Tamara have rapidly grown to become major players in the Buy Now, Pay Later (BNPL) market, attracting substantial international investment'

TABBY VERIFIED DETAILS:
- **Current Valuation**: $3.3 billion (February 2025)—Most valuable fintech in MENA
- **Latest Funding**: $160 million Series E (February 2025)
- **Previous Valuation**: $1.5 billion (late 2023)
- **Market Position**: Leading BNPL platform in Saudi Arabia, UAE, Kuwait
- **Unicorn Status**: Yes (achieved in 2023)

TAMARA VERIFIED DETAILS:
- **Current Valuation**: $1 billion (December 2023)—Saudi Arabia's first fintech unicorn
- **Latest Funding**: $340 million Series C (December 2023)
- **Market Position**: Leading BNPL platform in Saudi Arabia
- **Unicorn Status**: Yes (achieved December 2023)

SOURCES:
- TechCrunch, Reuters, Forbes reports
- Official company press releases
- Financial databases

GOVERNMENT VISION PROGRAMS VERIFICATION

SAUDI ARABIA VISION 2030

CLAIM: References to 'Saudi Arabia (Vision 2030)'

VERIFIED DETAILS:
- **Official Name:** Saudi Vision 2030 (correct)
- **Launch**: Officially launched by Saudi government
- **Scope**: Comprehensive economic, social, and cultural transformation plan
- **Key Objectives**: Economic diversification, reduced oil dependence, innovation promotion
- **Status**: Active and ongoing program
- **Official Website**: vision2030.gov.sa

UAE CENTENNIAL 2071

CLAIM: References to 'UAE (Centennial 2071)'

VERIFIED DETAILS:
- **Official Name**: UAE Centennial 2071 (correct)
- **Scope**: 50-year strategic plan extending to 2071
- **Launch**: Officially launched by UAE Cabinet
- **Objective**: Make UAE the best country in the world by 2071
- **Focus Areas**: Innovation, sustainability, global leadership
- **Official Source**: u.ae government portal.

MARKET ANALYSIS VERIFICATION

GCC STARTUP ECOSYSTEM CLAIMS

CLAIMS: Various statements about GCC market growth, government support, and investment climate

VERIFIED MARKET DATA (2024–2025):
- **GCC VC Funding Growth**: 19% CAGR from 2020–2024
- **2024 Total Deployed Capital**: $1.7 billion
- **Q1 2025 Performance**: $1.2 billion raised (strong start)
- **Average Deal Size Growth**: From $5.2M (Q1 2024) to $16.5M (Q1 2025)
- **Government Support**: Confirmed through multiple initiatives (Hub71, Monsha'at, etc.)

SOURCES:
- PwC Corporate Venture Capital Report 2025
- Startup Genome Global Ecosystem Report 2025
- Lucidity Insights market data
- Arabian Business reports.

AUTHOR BIO

Abdulrahman AlHammadi is a serial entrepreneur, investor, and mentor with over a decade of experience building and scaling successful ventures across the GCC region. As a founding partner of several technology startups and an advisor to multiple government innovation initiatives, he brings a unique perspective on the opportunities and challenges facing ambitious founders in the Gulf.

His passion for fostering the next generation of billion-dollar companies has led him to mentor hundreds of entrepreneurs and speak at prestigious events throughout the region. Through this book, he shares his proven methodology for building Uni-Camels—resilient, billion-dollar ventures adapted to thrive in the unique GCC ecosystem.

Abdulrahman holds degrees in Business Administration and Computer Science, and continues to actively invest in promising startups that align with the region's vision for economic diversification and technological advancement.

Connect with the Author:
Website: http://www.theunicamel.com
LinkedIn:
https://www.linkedin.com/in/abdulrahman-al-hammadi